THE POLAR WORLD

THE UNIQUE VISION OF SIR WALLY HERBERT

A *Polarworld* book

First published in Great Britain in 2007 by Polarworld

A CIP catalogue record for this book is available on request.

ISBN: 978-0-9555255-1-3

Printed in China by Imago Publishing Ltd

Polarworld
Edge Close
Weybridge
Surrey KT13 0SZ

www.polarworld.co.uk

*Editor's note: we use the term 'Eskimo' rather than 'Inuit' throughout to reflect the fact
that the people were known as the Polar Eskimos throughout the time Sir Wally Herbert
spent with them, and they still refer to themselves as Polar Eskimos as well as Inuit
(meaning 'The People').
Note also that we have tried wherever possible to ensure that the paintings, drawings and maps
are placed in such a way as to illustrate the text; however, due to the creative nature and content
of this book, some paintings may not be in a historically correct sequence.*

CONTENTS

FOR MARIE, KARI & PASCALE

WITH THANKS TO HURTIGRUTEN

FOR THEIR GENEROUS SUPPORT

Portrait of HRH The Prince of Wales (pencil & scalpel)

'This portrait of HRH The Prince of Wales was done as a token of thanks for his support and encouragement over the years.'

FOREWORD

CLARENCE HOUSE

Sir Wally Herbert (now at the age of 72), is quite rightly regarded as the doyen among polar explorers. He is, after all, one of the few remaining links we now have with that period of polar history known as the Heroic Age. Not only has he retraced the routes of most of the truly great pioneers both in the Arctic and the Antarctic during his fifty years as an explorer, but he has personally known a great many of them and, in turn, was greatly admired by them – so much so that Sir Raymond Priestley (the geologist on Shackleton's and Scott's Expeditions to the Antarctic) was one of the Vice-Patrons of Wally's Trans-Arctic Expedition in 1968-69, along with Lancelot Fleming, the Dean of Windsor, who had served as Geologist on the British Graham Land Expedition of 1934-37 – the last expedition to go to the Antarctic under sail and, with the exception of the Captain and Chief Engineer, an entirely amateur crew.

That expedition (in the three-masted topsail schooner *Penola*) had set out from St. Katherine's Dock in London on 10th September 1934, a few days before Wally was born, and as though destined to make a connection that would influence his choice of career, he had joined the choir of St. Chad's Church, Shrewsbury – the very church at which the curate was Norman Gurney (a "muscular Christian" if ever there was one) who had been b'osun on board *Penola* on her voyage to the Antarctic in 1934. Another of the sailors on that now historic voyage had been Duncan Carse (who at that time was a household name as the radio actor who played the role of 'Dick Barton Special Agent'). Wally was to be inspired by both of these men, particularly by the Antarctic curate who from the pulpit on Sunday mornings would enthral the choirboys and his congregation with tales of the *Penola* battling through the 'furious fifties' and the massive waves of the 'dreaded Drake Passage' on her way South to the Ice.

In his formative years, these were the seeds that were sown by good fortune and grew eventually into Wally's ambition to become a polar explorer. His dream, however, did not have its focus on a single goal – it was more in the nature of a 'call' or a mission. In this way his motives were somewhat different to those of his contemporaries, many of whom appeared to be driven by a fearsome obsession to be either the first or, failing that, the fastest. These motives, together with his extraordinary sensitivity to the polar environment, led to him and his three companions spending, uniquely, a long polar night on the drifting pack ice of the Arctic Ocean. They led him and his party to follow a route with their four teams of dogs in 1968-69 from Point Barrow in Alaska to Spitsbergen via the Pole of Inaccessibility (the point farthest from land on the Arctic Ocean) and the North Geographic Pole – a sixteen-month journey that completed the first surface crossing of the Arctic Ocean. Historically speaking, it was the last of the old-fashioned pioneering journeys on the face of the planet Earth – a journey during which there was no possibility of a rescue, from the first step to the last. No-one in the last thirty-six years has even attempted to re-trace that route. In today's world it is truly remarkable to consider that Wally has spent a total of fifteen years in the polar region, mapped vast areas of unexplored country and travelled with dog teams well over 25,000 miles.

His 'contribution' to our knowledge of that lonely, distant world goes far beyond the books he has written, and the maps and journeys he has made. He became almost at one with the wilderness as an explorer with an artist's eye – indeed, he is the only artist ever to have painted the Arctic and the Antarctic in all four seasons of the polar year from the perspective of the pioneer. Here then is a unique collection of some of Wally's evocative impressions of that polar world as he had the good fortune to find it.

INTRODUCTION

THE FIRST 15 YEARS OF MY POLAR CAREER was a journey for me of pure discovery in the 'heroic' and old-fashioned sense of the word – of travelling with dog teams in the Antarctic and mapping vast areas of unexplored country that no human being had set eyes on before. I was driven, at that time (as are most young explorers), by the dream of fame and a charming conviction that the world had been waiting with baited breath for me to show up and do my stuff. But by the time I had reached the North Pole with three companions and 40 dogs, this 'wind in my sails' had changed direction; I started upon a different sort of quest – an 'inner journey' if you like – and had started rereading the history books on which I had been raised.

What prompted this shift of consciousness, I cannot really say. Perhaps it was the experience of living and travelling with the Polar Eskimos, and learning from them how to tune in to Nature. Perhaps it was the influence of Laurens van der Post, who had urged me to look between the lines for what the explorers had kept to themselves – their secret sense of mission. Perhaps I was simply seeking a 'reason' for the many coincidences of date and place that had challenged and coloured my own career, for it was as though I had sensed some 'level of contact' with those explorers whose routes I had followed – Shackleton, Scott and Amundsen in the Antarctic and, at the opposite end of the world, the far more hazardous and wilder routes of Peary, Sverdrup and Dr Cook.

All I know is, the more deeply I searched within for answers to life's proverbial questions, the more I began to sense a link that joined all of those pioneers together in spite of the rivalry that existed between them. No longer did I see them as individuals, but as a group – a 'collective soul' – and from this point of view, my own contribution to the scheme of things started to fit in.

I now realized that each of these explorers (myself included) had been given only a part to play – a part of a collective mission to complete. Shackleton, for example, although a brilliant and charismatic leader of men, was destined to play the supporting role as the pathfinder to his rival Scott, who in turn was beaten to the South Pole by Amundsen (whose route I was the first to retrace exactly 50 years later). In the North there were of course scores of explorers (Nansen being the giant among them) who during the past 400 years had risked their lives in search of their goal, and each to a greater or lesser degree had contributed to our eventual attainment of the North Pole on 6 April 1969 – the 60th anniversary of Robert E. Peary's now totally discredited claim to priority that he made it there by the shorter route (and some truly impossible speeds).

There are still a few Peary supporters around (National Geographic being the most influential) who to this day refuse to listen to the arguments against his claim because they themselves were in awe of the man. The vast majority of polar historians and Pole-seeking adventurers of the present day, however, now credit my three companions and myself with being the first party of men to have reached the North Pole on foot, and every one of them now accepts that our journey with dogs across the top of the world from Alaska to Spitsbergen was not only the first surface crossing of the Arctic

Self-portrait No. 2 (pencil & scalpel)

Ocean, but also the last of the great pioneering journeys made on the face of the Earth.

It was a journey hailed by the then-Prime Minister, Harold Wilson, as a 'feat of endurance and courage which ranks with any in polar history', and an achievement in the opinion of HRH Prince Philip (the Patron of the Expedition) that 'ranks among the greatest triumphs of human skill and endurance'. It was also a journey that, somewhat strangely, triggered a whole series of coincidences.

Besides the coincidence of reaching the North Pole on 6 April, there was the equally amazing coincidence that after a trek of 3,800 route miles (a journey that took 16 months to complete) we touched land on 29 May 1969 – at the same GMT, and on exactly the 16th anniversary of Sir Edmund Hillary and Sherpa Tensing reaching the summit of Mount Everest – a coincidence that completed the 'trilogy' of the first ascent of the world's highest mountain, and the first surface crossing of the southern and the northern ice caps of the world.

But perhaps the most meaningful of coincidences from that period of my life was the one of which I did not even become aware until several years later. I had been looking at an atlas of the moon by Patrick Moore in which

there was a picture of the *Earthrise* – that very famous picture in which the Earth is seen rising from behind the barren lunar horizon. The caption said that the picture was taken on the Apollo 10 mission in May 1969 – the mission on which Astronaut John 'Jack' Young was the pilot of the Command Module. That the picture had been taken in May 1969 intrigued me, so I wrote to Jack Young, and his reply confirmed that at the exact same GMT that we had sighted land, he had taken that fantastic picture. It was one of the most powerful images that mankind had ever seen, and that those two events are linked is surely of some significance. Certainly within my own close circle of colleagues and friends the synchronicity of those two events clearly marked the moment in time when one period of exploration came to an end and a new one boldly began.

In the 35 years since that day in May 1969, several astronauts have walked on the moon, and several scores of adventurers have sledged, skied, or snowmobiled by the shorter route to the North Pole. At the opposite end of the Earth (at the time of writing), the South Pole has been reached by no fewer than 200 individuals, most of whom have flown home from there, and Mount Everest has been climbed by at least 1,500 mountaineers since Hillary and Tensing made the first ascent in 1953! And yet, in spite of all this record-breaking and glory-seeking no one in the past 35 years has ever repeated, or even attempted to repeat, our journey across the longest axis of the Arctic Ocean, nor has anyone been prepared to live through the awesome experience of 16 months of isolation on the drifting polar pack. In fact, these days we seem to be breeding a different type of polar 'explorer' – men and women who love adventure, but who insist their adventures should be short and 'extreme'.

Perhaps they can see the 'writing on the wall' – that every journey to the Pole must now be done at breakneck speed because, half a dozen years from now, 'global warming' will seriously have reduced the amount of ice that is afloat on the Arctic Ocean. How ironic that the ice thickness data against which scientists these days are measuring the changes affecting the climates of the world are based on the ice and pressure ridge measurements provided by Dr 'Fritz' Koerner, the glaciologist of that four-man expedition which made the historic trek with dogs across the top of the world in 1968-69.

During the 15 years that followed the so-called 'high point' in my polar career (as is often the case with men and women who set or seek new physical boundaries by which to live), I returned to the Arctic determined to make an even longer and more hazardous journey than the one I had made across the North Pole. I got married on Christmas Eve during the final crazy days of the 60s, then with my bride and baby daughter (who was only a few months old at that time) travelled to the extreme Northwest of Greenland to live with the Polar Eskimos for two years. I had been driven by the example of the documentary film-maker Robert Flaherty, who (entirely alone) had made a film of the Eskimos in the Canadian Arctic called *Nanook of the North*, and during that time in Greenland I sledged several thousands of miles with some of the finest long-range hunters of the world's most northerly Inuit tribe.

That period spent with the hunters of the polar bear, and the sense of isolation I experienced during the attempt to make the first circumnavigation of Greenland with Allan Gill (who had been with me on the North Pole crossing in 1968–69) was a 'conquest' of the unknown in certain respects, and yet, at a far more personal level, it was a spiritual bonding with the polar wilds – an awakening of the soul. It was as though I was being prepared and honed for the final phase of this lifetime.

Right up to this time (some 30 years into my career as a polar explorer), I had refused to accept that I had an untrained 'gift' for painting – that I had, in a sense, been an 'artist in waiting' for well over 40 years of my life. True enough, my art teacher at school had insisted that I had an aptitude for drawing portraits and should seriously consider entering this speciality as one of the subjects in my School Certificate examination. I had reluctantly agreed, being the only one in the school to be singled out in this way and fearing the

attention I would attract by being cooped up alone with a professional model for some time – although on this last argument I need not have worried for the model's fees were considered too high and the school's cleaning lady was persuaded to sit for me instead.

She was a dear old crone with a hard life deeply engraved in her face – actually, a far more attractive proposition for a portrait artist than a younger sitter would have been. But the old lady – no doubt marvelling at how easy life had suddenly become (where all she was required to do in order to be paid a few shillings was to sit still) – was soon fast asleep and gently snoring. How long she was 'away' I do not know – I was far too engrossed with my drawing. But I guess it must have been some time, for the drawing had reached the stage where there was a very definite likeness appearing.

It was at that moment – the most exciting and decisive moment in any portrait – that the old lady crumpled in the middle like a rag doll, slid from her perch, and hit the hard wooden floor with a sickening thud. 'She's dead,' I thought 'and I'm to blame' – and by the time she had recovered, all interest in the idea of becoming an artist had completely disappeared.

This decision really was a tremendous relief. There would be time enough to indulge my 'gift' when I was an old man and too weak to continue my search for a mission. Then I could, with a clear conscience, seek out this other form of self-expression – one that ran parallel but perhaps a little deeper than the beautifully chosen word.

This other form of self-expression of which I speak is of course my painting, and the reason for publishing this book. On reflection, I could not help but notice that I had been an artist in waiting for so long. All the paintings I had done since I made the discovery that I could paint in 1989 have been based on memory, or photographs, and with the former (in my case) being less reliable than the latter, I prefer the photograph as my reminder. Of course I change the composition or the detail in the painting as I see fit, but it is only fair to point out that all the paintings in this book are therefore, by definition, retrospective. This presents no problem in a gallery where the paintings are seen and judged purely on their artistic merit; but here the text or the caption dictates where the picture should fit into the composition of the book as a whole, and the text, generally speaking, has to flow in chronological order. This is particularly so with this book, which in a sense is autobiographical – starting with the first intimation of the life that lay ahead for me and progressing through a polar career, from one expedition to another, almost to the present day.

The paintings in this book are therefore an expression of what I have seen, felt, and experienced many times over, and through all of the seasons in the Polar World.

KEEN YOUNG MEN

'I was now in territory that was familiar to me from the books of the pioneering explorers, Scott and Shackleton, who had penetrated the Ross Sea in the early part of the 20th century in search of a place to land. Yet no amount of knowledge had prepared me for the experience of seeing the pack ice for the first time and hearing the sounds of the ice creaking under pressure from our little wooden ship.'

WALLY HERBERT, 1968

I REMEMBER VERY LITTLE ABOUT MY CHILDHOOD. I had been told, of course, of various events to which I had made some contribution during the first few bruising years of my life. But so few of these appear to have registered, and I came to the conclusion quite early that being a boy was a waste of time – that mine was an 'adult mission'.

Any psychologist worth his salt would probably have considered these missing events of interest, perhaps even of some relevance – such as my first serious adventure of walking across a frozen river on ice that was barely thick enough to support the weight of a boy of 12 – the very first 'triumph' of my life that I can recall. I remember especially returning home and boasting proudly about what I had done and of my parents' angry reaction – my mother weeping (I presumed with relief) and my father in an alarming rage because we had only recently been reunited after a separation during the war years and he did not know whether his role as a father and a military man gave him the right to beat me. I find it ironic (in retrospect) that my final thrashing as a boy should have been for the very act of walking on ice that appeared, several years later, to be part of my destiny.

Delivered to Dover

My father had been born into a family of which every male member during the past 400 years had served his country as a soldier, and he was a great believer in the rule of law and in the virtue of self-discipline. He was particularly proud of his heritage – and even more proud of being the eldest son of a sergeant in the regiment of the South Wales Borderers – one hundred of whose men had fought at the famous battle of Rorke's Drift in

1879 during the Anglo-Zulu War (immortalized in the Hollywood film *Zulu* starring the actor Michael Caine). No fewer than 11 Victoria Crosses were won 'For Valour' in the fight on that tiny battlefield – the battle where more VCs were won than in any other in history. My grandfather had obviously been inspired by this heroism to join the same regiment and had distinguished himself by twice being 'Mentioned in Despatches'. He had died at the early age of 39 while serving in South Africa, and his widow (an army school mistress with six small children of her own) had sent her eldest son back to England from Cape Town at the age of nine with a label sewn on to the front of his jersey saying 'deliver this boy to the Duke of York's Royal Military School at Dover'.

My father later told me about his first day on the parade ground of the school for the orphans of soldiers. How, on that bitterly cold day in November dressed only in shorts, he was singled out and beaten by the sergeant major for snivelling and shivering with cold. He even proudly showed me in later years the first letter he received from his mother: '… We hope you like your soldier's cloths and keep your boots and buttons polished. And remember: you are a soldier now, and try to be a man.' This to a boy of only nine years of age! And yet in spite of this brutal start to his life in the army, he would never hear a word against it, and at the age of 13 he was enlisted into the Royal Regiment of Artillery.

He never spoke about his courtship – although I understand he was a lodger in the house in which my mother was the youngest daughter of a large family of simple country folk. From my mother, however, I learnt that his proposal of marriage had been written on a note that he pushed under the door of her room as he set off to join a troop ship bound for China. There he was to serve for the next four years climbing slowly through the ranks, collecting laurels for himself and his regiment as a brilliant army sportsman, and building up a most impressive scrapbook in that time of press clippings and cartoons praising his achievements.

My parents married on my father's return from China and I was born on 24 October l934 in a tiny terraced house in the City of York. I am therefore regarded as a Yorkshireman, although, in truth, I was only in that neighbourhood for about two months before being taken on a troop ship to Egypt.

There my younger sister was born in l939, and shortly after the outbreak of the Second World War my mother, baby sister and I were evacuated out of the 'War Zone' on a ship heading south through the Suez Canal in the only direction safe at the time. Along with several other soldiers' families, we were put ashore in South Africa and told to fend for ourselves until the war was over.

It was there, on a ranch in the Drakensberg Mountains, that I spent a somewhat strange and solitary childhood – a fatherless existence without any companions of my own in a wild and remote region. I had no male adults to discipline me, or offer me any encouragement. My sister and I did not meet the 'stranger' who was supposed to be our father until after the war had ended and it was difficult for all of us to adjust. From the start he insisted that I call him 'Sir' and that I should go to the same school where he had learned to swim by being bodily thrown into the deep end. This I stubbornly refused to do, or to keep in step with him later in life – and of course I deeply regret that I did not swallow my pride and accept this military bearing in him.

Signing Up

For many years I resisted the collective pressure from my father and two of his surviving brothers that I should join the army when I left school. This, they had assured me, was as close as I could ever get to becoming an explorer – I could join the Survey Branch of the Royal Engineers, and on secondment to the ex-Colonial countries in Africa I could join border survey and mapping projects in virtually unknown territory. I had been given the same advice by the careers advisory service in my final year at school. And so, naively, at the age of 17 I was marched off to the nearest Army Recruiting Office escorted by three officers in uniform and signed up for 22 years.

True, my contract gave me an option of leaving the army after serving only three years, but the advantage of me being a 'career soldier' was that I could be eligible for special courses – such as those at the School of Military Survey,

which would give me a grounding in cartography and navigation (qualifications I would need if I was, eventually, to become an explorer).

This is pretty much the way it worked out. I spent a year at the School of Military Survey and was then posted out to Egypt and there in a tented camp in the Suez Canal Zone I spent the next two years producing maps of Kenya from air photos and counting the grains of sand in the desert. But this did not fulfil me and I managed to persuade the colonel that I had more to offer life as a civilian. Surprisingly, he agreed, and so I left the army in Egypt and hitchhiked back to England drawing portraits for my board and lodging and, as often as not, sleeping rough. From Cyprus I had taken a nightmare steerage passage on a stinking old ship across to the coast of Turkey and then through Greece and Italy I made my way from one loss of dignity straight to another – a stream of adventures in the space of five months that aged me by as many years.

Actually that ageing process was to work distinctly to my advantage sooner than I imagined, although for the first few months after my return I could see no glimmer of light at the end of my black tunnel of despair – there seemed to be no possibility whatsoever of becoming the explorer I yearned to be. I took a job as a cartographer with an air survey company on the south coast of England, working a night shift so that I could have the summer sunshine to laze in – and I lazed away my free hours dreaming.

A World of Men

'Seaward with my hopes went matchsticks, whirling downstream, past the seagulls that were pecking at their plump reflections. Shoreham-by-Sea bustled not far away. A church bell clanged the hour of day, marking the passage of wasted time. I was alone – a morose young man, burdened by the awful frustration of wanting so much to be an explorer, yet not knowing how to become one.'

These were the words with which I opened *A World of Men* – my naive and embarrassingly gushing first book. I went on to describe how chance had offered a timely hand:

'It was a blustery day, and the lurching bus taking me to work was dank with the odour of steaming raincoats. I had paid my fare, lit my pipe, and had just closed my eyes, when there was a rush of wind, and in my lap a newspaper lay that had fallen from the luggage rack. It was opened at the Public Appointments page, and as I wrestled to turn the page over, two advertisements caught my eye almost simultaneously: "Surveyor required in Kenya," one said – "Expedition to Antarctica" said the other!

"The Falklands Dependency Survey, which maintains isolated land bases on the Antarctic, requires SURVEYORS. Candidates, SINGLE, must be keen young men of good education and high physical standard, who have a genuine interest in Polar research and travel, and are willing to spend 30 months under conditions which are a test of character and resource. Salary 330 pounds (Sterling). Write to Crown Agents, 4 Millbank, London S.W.1."

'I jumped off the bus, ran past the boat yards, over the bridge and along by the mud banks. I arrived at work in a glow, borrowed a pen, secluded myself in the smallest room and wrote an application for each of the jobs. I was in an agony of excitement as the days went by. Then I was summoned to London for an interview. But it did not seem to go very well – I arrived for the interview panting for breath having followed an ageing commissionaire up several flights of stairs. I could feel myself sweating, and jokingly waved my arm in the direction of the door suggesting that the three men who were waiting for me should take the much fitter commissionaire on the expedition instead. My light-hearted opening to the interview, however, was met with the rebuff: "Sit down Mr Herbert – we haven't much time."

'For all the questions they asked I should have had answers – simple questions I might have known would come up, such as: "Why do you want to go to the Antarctic?" A searching question if ever there was one – and yet all I could splutter on the spur of the moment was, "Because I've always wanted to go there". I felt very foolish.

'Right from the time I was a smooth-skinned choirboy in St Chads' Church, Shrewsbury, my hero and role model had been the Rev. Norman Gurney. He was a strapping young curate, fresh from college, who had sailed to the Antarctic as bosun on the three-masted topsail schooner *Penola*, from St Katherine's Dock in London on 10 September 1934, a few days before I was born. Clearly I had been destined to join that particular choir and to be influenced by his sermons on Sunday mornings when he would enthral us choirboys and his congregations with tales of the *Penola* battling through the "Furious Fifties" and the massive waves of the Drake Passage on her way south to the ice. Another member of the crew had been Duncan Carse who at the time of my youth had been a household name as the radio actor who played the role of "Dick Barton Special Agent". In my formative years these were the two men I most greatly admired, and I had read every book I could lay my hands on in preparation for the time I would follow their example. Why then had I not mentioned this influence?

"If you were tent-bound for ten days or more, how would you keep your tent mates amused?" That one completely beat me. But why did I not, there and then, tell them of some of the amazing adventures I had recently had on my journey home from Egypt?

"I'm sorry, Mr Herbert, but we really don't think you are suitable," the man in the grey suit said, and my heart sank with a thud. And they were just about to draw a line through my name on their list of applicants when I boldly demanded to know their reasons. They all looked up from their pads with surprise.

"Well, Mr Herbert, it's like this: we are interested in what a man has done – not what a man says he would like to do. You haven't done very much with your life so far, have you?"

"No Sir, I suppose not," I said totally crestfallen. I tried to be polite and say "Good Morning", but the words got stuck in my throat, so I simply stood up and walked out. There were surely some lessons to be learnt from that interview – the obvious one being to give the interviewer enough information to make a fair assessment. Sure enough, I was still only 20 years of age and had no professional qualifications – and this struck me very hard when I returned to the waiting room where my fellow applicants were seated. All of them had degrees and were at least five years older than me, but not one of them had done anything with their lives to prove that they had spirit and a powerful sense of destiny. I had both, but had failed to point it out – or so at least I thought, until they sent the commissionaire after me as I was walking away from the ordeal with the message that I was to go right away to Harley Street for a medical.'

Setting Sail

So, clearly I had come through, and I was overjoyed. Two months later I was standing among a herd of 'keen young men' on board the Royal Research Ship *Shackleton* at Berth 37 Southampton Dock and we were about to cast off. It was a cold and rainy 27 December 1955. We were following a few weeks in the wake of The Commonwealth Trans-Antarctic Expedition ship the *M.V. Theron*, but the sounds of a sea port paid us no attention: no sirens or church bells bade us farewell; only a few friends and relations were waving their handkerchiefs tearfully as they stood on the quay mirrored in puddles of water.

It was a long voyage down through the Atlantic, calling only at Cape Verde Islands and Montevideo before feeling the full force of the "Roaring Forties" en-route to Port Stanley in the Falkland Islands. There we spent a few days stevedoring cargo from the *Shackleton* to the old *John Biscoe*. Again we were interviewed to decide which base we would go to, and for me there was only one that had the truly heroic dog-sledging tradition – Hope Bay at the northernmost tip of the Peninsula. My delight was therefore complete when I was transferred to the old *John Biscoe* for a passage to Hope Bay, which was to be my base for the next two years, and the central plateau of the Peninsula to be my mapping territory.

The voyage from here was very special, for I was now in territory that was familiar to me from the books of the pioneering explorers, Scott and

Shackleton, who had penetrated the Ross Sea in the early part of the 20th century in search of a place to land, and of course the sermons and private stories of my role-model curate, Norman Gurney of St Chad's - the bosun of the last sailing vessel of the 'Heroic Age' to operate in these waters. Yet no amount of knowledge had prepared me for the experience of seeing the pack ice for the first time and hearing the sounds of the ice creaking under pressure from our little wooden ship.

Arriving at Duce Bay

We sailed all day through the pack ice on our fifth day south from Stanley around the coast to Duce Bay where we were to land the building materials at View Point for a four-man hut we would erect later in the year. That evening a curtain of cloud was drawn across the sky, leaving only a chink of brilliant light along the western seaboard. It caught the frayed cloud base in waves of crimson and purple and this was reflected in the sea-lanes between the ice floes. To the east, night had already settled, and by the time we reached Duce Bay it was dark.

No ship had ever been in that bay before, and the captain was disinclined to break a channel through the old bay ice towards the previously chosen site of the new hut on View Point, which was difficult to see from the ship even with the searchlight trained on it. The area was well-known for its winds and strong currents, and so the passengers and crew were divided into two working parties, one of which would be shipbound, working the stores from the hold to the deck and then into the scow, while the other group would work ashore, off-loading the stores onto a rocky headland about a mile and a half from the hut site. I was detailed to go with the shore party, by which time the night was almost pitch black, with just the occasional flash from the ship's searchlight – conditions that made for a very dramatic first landing in the Antarctic.

The scow bucked in the swell and scraped on the rocks – mooring lines tightened and then went slack tripping us up as we struggled with the cumbersome loads. We crawled like ants over the greasy boulders, supporting each other, or forming a chain to pass the sandbags and heavy crates, occasionally all of us coming together to handle an awkward load across slippery planks bridging the surging tide between the scow's gunwale and the sea-sprayed rocks. The ship's searchlight would feel its way along the coast,

Hope Bay at the Time of Leaving (watercolour) [pages 24–25]

find us, then wander away. For a moment we would recognize each other, then in darkness again we would fumble about.

Eventually the job was done and most of the men went back to the ship for a well-earned short break. Major Ellery Anderson and I, however, decided to stay ashore. He had just completed his time as base leader of Hope Bay and in that time had made a very fine dog-sledging journey of a thousand miles down the east coast, mapping much new country. Within a couple of weeks he would be back in Stanley where he would be rudely jolted back into the civilized world. For me it was exciting to meet for the first time a real explorer in this own environment and, not wishing to break the spell, I respectfully just listened to his stories.

Major Anderson's hooked pipe burned brightly bathing his face in a macabre glow – a moving mask with highlights shifting all the time. Beyond lay a sombre backdrop of deep grey hills, very faintly outlined against a bleached horizon, while overhead I was vaguely aware of the closeness of cloud, tumbling slowly in an almost imperceptible breeze. The sea was a pool of black ink, lapping around the rocks below us, and the *John Biscoe*, with her well-deck ablaze with yellow light, lay off the headland. It was a magical night – and quite a long time before the next scow arrived.

In the weak light of early morning with the hut stores all safely landed, the *John Biscoe* weaved her way through the pack ice around the coast of Hope Bay. I confess I slept for most of the way for it had been a hard but memorable night, and I did not come out of that deep sleep until the anchor was dropped in the bay – my home base for the next two and a half years. As I ducked through the door out onto the deck I was confronted with a scene to delight the eyes: an ambush of towering pyramids, blade ridges and scooped snow corries; a sky slashed by frayed ribbons of cloud flung by an invisible hand; a pool full of inverted mountains jostling for space among the chattering chunks of ice.

Andersson, Duce and Grunden

It must have been much the same for the three men in my drawing (*see page 18*) – the first three men to spend a winter at Hope Bay. Their names were Dr Gunnar Andersson, Lieutenant Duce and Seaman Toralf Grunden. They had landed there 53 years earlier as the relief party for Otto Nordenskjöld's

Swedish South Polar Expedition of l901–03, which had set up its base at Snow Hill Island. With six companions, Nordenskjöld had spent the previous winter there and had undertaken some amazing exploratory journeys down the east coast of the Antarctic Peninsula.

At the spot we called 'Last Hill', overlooking a breathtaking view across Duce Bay towards the hut we would build on the far side of the bay, Gunnar Andersson had written in glowing terms of the same view: 'We stand silent and perplexed, and gaze at the new and wonderful scene. Mile upon mile of snowy plain, such as we have never seen before, meets our eyes; one can actually imagine that a gigantic snow-clad city lies before us, with houses and palaces in thousands, and in hundreds of changing, irregular forms – towers and spires, and all the wonders of the world.' He went on, 'I have never before been able even

Andersson, Duce & Grunden (pencil & scalpel) *'Gunnar Andersson, Lieutenant Duce and Seaman Toralf Grunden – the first three men to spend a winter at Hope Bay.'*

to imagine such a picture of the sovereign dominion of ice, as the one offered by this landscape.'

Gunnar Andersson was a geologist and went on his first serious walkabout the day after he returned from his sledging expedition, and was excited to find indistinct fossils of ferns in a block of stone. It was evident that he had discovered fossil flora from the Triassic or Jurassic systems, quite a new find in the South Polar regions, and one of immense importance for a determination of the former climate of the earth.

One of the most significant things about their wintering was their good humour and their unfailing optimism considering the dire circumstances in which they found themselves when the ship sent to pick them up failed to materialize and they were forced to winter at Hope Bay, surviving on the few seals and birds they managed to hunt. They were always polite and civil and respectful of the space that each man needed. As Gunnar Andersson put it: 'There never existed amongst us any unforgiving, ever increasing ill-will of which so much is related in the accounts of other winterings under far more

fortunate circumstances.' There is a lot that the modern adventurer could learn from these old explorers and I had the most profound admiration for them.

Finally they left the remains of their hut and, nearing Cape Dreyfus (since renamed Cape Well-Met for very obvious reasons), they encountered what they had first mistaken for seals – except that these were vertical! As they approached, as Gunnar Andersson recalls: 'the Greenland dogs make a dash to one side on catching sight of the two wild men'. Nordenskjöld's confusion was total. 'Black as soot from head to toe; men with black clothes, black faces and high black caps, and with their eyes hidden by peculiar wooden frames … my powers of guessing fail me, when I endeavour to imagine to what race of men these creatures belong.'

These three men were heroes as far as we, the 'keen young men' of Hope Bay, were concerned, and as we gazed out at the scene from the *John Biscoe* we felt immensely proud to be a part of its history.

Mount Taylor dominated the picture, and small wisps of cloud drifting out of its shadow puffed alight in the sun like silent shell bursts above Depot Glacier, while Mount Flora, majestically crinolined in scree, preened herself in the mirror at her feet. On either side of us, like gigantic waves, smooth snowfields dipped steeply into the bay, staining the waterline almost black with a tidemark of bare rock. The floating ice was drifting by. It was jingling and knocking on the sides of our ship, and the dust of sunbeams played in the water like pricks of light among the chunks of brash.

The Hut at Hope Bay

No building has ever meant so much to me as that timber hut at Hope Bay. It was steeped in character. The traditional design of the bunkhouse living-quarters resembled the system instituted by Shackleton in his Cape Royds hut at McMurdo Sound. Like Shackleton's hut, our bunkhouse was one big room

The Hut at Hope Bay
(pen & ink)

full of atmosphere, with the beds head-to-toe around the walls and a fireplace near the middle, but unlike Shackleton's men we were not permitted to build partitions, and so lacked even the modicum of privacy. This did not upset us – on the contrary, I believe it was partly responsible for strengthening our 'expedition spirit'. What inspired us more, however, was our library (one whole wall of polar books) and the legacy of intrepid journeys that had been made from this base by our predecessors over the years since the first base had been built at Hope Bay in 1945 as part of a British Naval expedition under the wartime codename Operation Tabarin.

The first base leader had been Major Andrew Taylor of the Royal Canadian Engineers and the many journeys they made were fascinating reading in their official reports. The leadership then fell to Captain Vic Russell. It was he who discovered the route to the plateau that we were eventually to follow in 1957, and many of his pioneering maps were used by us during our time. In 1947 Frank Elliott took charge, and during his first winter he made a one-way sledging journey of 700 miles with three companions down the east coast of the peninsula, from where he was given a passage back to Hope Bay by the annual supply ship.

Frank Elliott was one of the three men who sat on the interview panel before which I went at the Crown Agents and was no doubt responsible for selecting me – for which I will be forever grateful.

Two men, however, tragically lost their lives in a fire at the base during Frank's time, and the base was for a short while closed. This encouraged the Argentine Government to build their own base at Hope Bay, and Dr George March had been the one who ran the gauntlet of the Argentines' spirited defenders of what they regarded as Argentine Antarctic Territory when he and his men built the new British base called Trinity House up on the hill. For two years he was leader, and he and his men made many long journeys of exploration in their time, at the end of which he joined the Ross Sea Party of the Commonwealth Trans-Antarctic Expedition as the medical officer and their expert dog driver.

Finally, there were two other Hope Bay men of note, David Statton and his fellow surveyor Ken Blaiklock, members of Dr Fuchs' party, which made the historic first surface crossing of the Antarctic. So we felt proudly represented by all of these men even before we had fully become Hope Bay men ourselves.

How well I remember that hut, coal black against a big white hill, with its stiff flag flying and its chimney in a howling gale. It was a shell of pine timbers that creaked and groaned, with big double windows down either side and guy wires that passed right over the roof every 10 feet throughout its length and anchored the structure to solid rock. It would not have been a handsome hut in any other setting, but it had a certain majesty in its stark simplicity, and the rows of upturned sledges neatly parked down the leeward side gave it the distinctive character of a British polar base.

There was a door at either end, and the more pleasant entrance of the two was the downwind or northeast door below the tattered flag. It opened into a narrow room aromatic with the sledging smells of raw linseed oil and tautening dope, beeswax, ropes, and lampwick harnesses, each marked with the name of a dog and reeking with its sweat. To the left in racks against the wall were found sets of skis and bamboo sticks, while to the right hung alpine ropes and oiled ice axes, crevasse probes, dog whips and centre traces. Sledging chattels filled the shelves and littered the benches at the far end of the room, evoking an impression of a ship's chandlery store stocked with such a diversity of gear that only initiated men would have known what each item was for.

It was a room full of atmosphere, and to the left of it was a passageway, three paces long, like a tunnel between one cave and another. Blood-stained anoraks grisly with seal's hair, and felling axes greasy with blubber hung on either side of this passageway, while on a low shelf in one corner sat an open bucket that served as a urinal when the weather was foul. So it was not the sweetest-smelling part of the hut, and nor was the room to which that passage gave access, for the carpenter's shop with its boiler stove roaring was next to the generator room with its smells of oil and diesel fumes.

The carpenter's shop was the preserve of no man in particular, although I cannot think of that room without picturing a lean and intense ex-sailor by the name of Pat Thompson. He was an exceptionally skilled craftsman with a sailor's traditional love of model-making, and this, combined with the more unusual passion for classical music, had produced a need in Pat during his second winter to make a violin – an ambitious piece of carpentry that had very soon become the focal point of Trinity House.

Even our friends from the Argentine base had filed like pilgrims through the sledge workshop to pay their respects to the mute instrument that, resembling a small dismembered body, lay for weeks on the workshop table. But in time it had become the bane of our lives, and on the day that its belly peg slipped, we dared not even glance in its direction as we hurried through the workshop to and from the washroom. As for the dramatic end to Pat's plywood violin – that

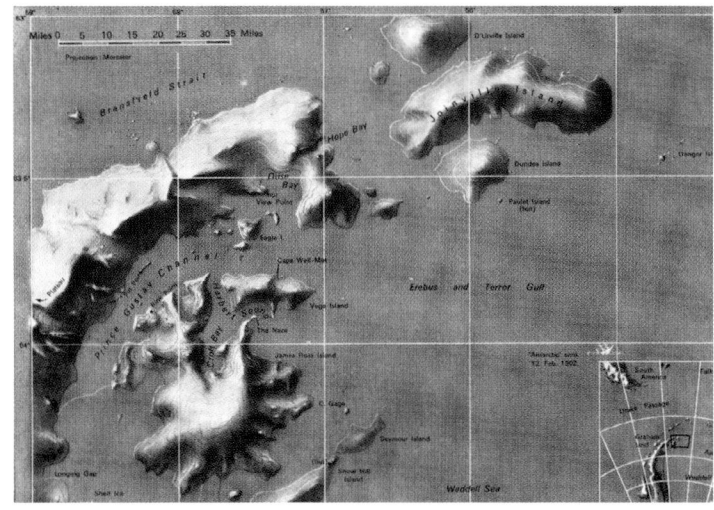

'My map showing the territory over which the 12 men at Hope Bay travelled with dog teams during the period 1955–58.'

came a few days later when in a moment of intense frustration he had smashed it to smithereens.

Reluctant Artist

Such moments of high emotion, however, were rare in our society. Indeed, this passion of Pat's for his violin was the only hobby actively followed in my time on base. Even in my own case, I had kept it a secret that I had brought with me from home my old school paintbox and three small brushes in the hope discreetly of being able to record my impressions when no one else was looking. Why this reticence? In almost every other aspect, our lives at Hope Bay had been modelled on the traditions laid down by Captain Scott in 1911–1912. Dr Edward Wilson, the Chief Scientist and Naturalist on two of Scott's Antarctic Expeditions, had no such scruples and certainly no embarrassment in spending much of his spare time painting what he called 'watercolour sketches' with a meticulous eye for detail. His paintings undeniably were a useful contribution to the record of the expedition (particularly since colour photography was in its infancy in the early years of the 20th century). But the role of the artist, particularly in the Polar World, has always been on shaky ground because painting was seen by the ordinary seaman as an excuse on the part of the 'officer artists' to be relieved from the drudgery of menial chores and be left conscience-free to create.

The death of Dr Wilson and his four companions on their homeward journey from the South Pole brought this period of history to an end, and by 1955, when I went south for the first time, any period spent painting was seen as a waste – an activity that should be reserved for when an explorer was old and infirm, and not a moment sooner.

At that time I entirely accepted this ruling, for my mission in life (so I then believed) was to be an explorer – to make maps of those areas of the Antarctic that had never before been seen by man, and the first of the many maps I made during the 1950s and early 60s was the map (*left*) showing the territory over which the 12 men at Hope Bay travelled with dog teams during the period 1955–58

It was published as an illustration for my first book, *A World of Men*, and adopted a medium used by cartographers at that time for producing a three-dimensional effect known by them as 'hill shading'. The technique was more artistic than technical – the effect being

achieved by drawing the map on a sheet of white astrofoil that had been sprayed with a grey printer's ink. The mountains and hills on the map were then shaded on the 'dark' side with a soft lead pencil, while the sun-facing side of the hill (*top left of picture*) was scraped clean of ink with a surgeon's scalpel. As a mapping medium it was fairly short-lived, for within a few years other ways had been found of producing this result. But fortunately I had come upon it at a time when it had served as a link between the explorer and the creative spirit, and over the next few years I made several drawings using this medium – most of them portraits based on the photos of the men whose paths had crossed with mine, and some on meditations that became jacket covers for synopses of books I have yet to write.

The moment of inspiration – when the paint started flowing – came about in 1989, a few months after the publication of my ninth book, the biography of Cdr Robert E. Peary entitled *The Noose of Laurels*. The book had been deeply stressful to write, because of the empathy I had for the man, and it was a while before I had recovered sufficiently even to consider writing again. But since giving up my active career as a polar explorer in 1980, I had officially considered myself a writer by profession – and so I set about producing two book synopses: one entitled *Nine Lives* and the other a novel set in Greenland called *King Dog*. Both of these synopses, however, went the rounds of 13 publishers without receiving even the slightest show of interest from any of them, and this of course was deeply upsetting for me – particularly as these were the best-written and best-presented synopses I had ever produced.

At that point Marie, who had by then had become a psychotherapist, offered me some advice: 'try your hand at painting, it may relieve your stress'. I frankly found this hard to believe since I had not used my old school paintbox for at least 38 years, and was worried that my stress might be further increased if the painting was a disaster.

But the first two paintings seemed to be blessed by pure luck. The first was a watercolour of the Eskimo hunter Avatak (my main travelling companion in Northwest Greenland in 1971–73) standing on a pressure ridge in the middle of Smith Sound scanning the horizon for polar bears.

The second was a watercolour of the same hunter on a midwinter's journey I had made with him and our two teams of dogs, *South to Find the Sun*. It was based on a black and white photo I had taken on a journey we had made from Herbert Island to Savissivik on the north coast of Melville Bay in Northwest Greenland. Travelling almost entirely in darkness we had camped at the entrance of a cave – memorable mainly for its acoustic triple echo, and the fact that it had been used by most of the explorers who had lived in that region, notably Peary, Freuchen and Rasmussen.

But it was the purity of the third painting that called me to put down the brushes and ask the question 'where is it coming from?' This painting (also a watercolour) I had called *The Ice Bear*.

The circumstances under which it was painted were horrendous: we were living in those days through one of our 'lean times' in a small bungalow with a tiny garden shed at the back. I had rigged it up with electricity for heating and lighting and converted it into a cramped studio. But during the three days I was working on the painting there was a storm that nearly took the roof off and a torrential downpour, which came though the roof in a stream of water that had to be directed with a rubber groundsheet (suspended from the roof beams with climbing rope and sagging with the weight of the rain water) into a bucket alongside the work. Just one splash, of course, would have ruined the painting.

'I think your watercolour is brilliant.
How you do it I can't imagine – it is sheer genius.'

HRH The Prince of Wales

The Vision

But that painting was also memorable because of the 'vision' I had as soon as the painting was finished. Call it a 'dream' if you prefer, but either way, in my meditation, I found myself alone in a preview theatre watching a showing of colour slides of paintings – all (except one) on a 'polar' theme, and all by an

South, to Find the Sun

(watercolour)

'Avatak – my main travelling companion in Northwest Greenland – and I had travelled south to Savissivik, a good 200 miles south of Thule, to watch the sun return after the long months of winter darkness. Our plan was to see the sun then race the sun back to our village and tell our wives what it was like. We only just made it back in time as the sun was coming back rather quickly at that latitude. But that was the theory: that we would travel south to bring the sun back with us.'

The Ice Bear (watercolour)
[pages 28–29]

unknown artist. The paintings, however, were vaguely familiar, and some of them were of polar scenes that only I had seen. At this point in the slide-show I had become intrigued as to who was the painter whose work I was viewing, and what was the date he had finished the work, and on looking closer I was truly astonished to see my own signature on every painting and a date of completion that in a few cases was three years into the future!

What I had in effect been shown was a colour preview of the first 26 works that I would complete – a period of 'learning' I had presumed, since I was entirely self-taught as a painter. As for the painting of Mount Everest (which was in itself surprising enough since I had not physically been to the base camp of Everest): beyond that slide the screen went black, and it struck me that this was ominous – that there would be no paintings beyond this.

I had also been shown by the 'vision' that the historical pictures, rather than exact copies of the photographs, were instead reminders of what the photographer had seen. As a creative artist, I would later argue, I was entitled to use my years of polar experience to show the same scene in a slightly different way – for example, if the sky in the photograph was black (indicating that the picture was taken when the sky was cloudless and the photographer was using a yellow filter), I could, quite legitimately, alter it to add colour or cloud if the picture needed more interest or dramatic effect. Indeed, it is a well-known fact that Frank Hurley (the photographer on Shackleton's *Endurance* Expedition) made adjustments to many of his famous images. In effect my own 'adjustments' also gave me a 'say' in what the painting was trying to portray – as though, in some cases, I was there (alongside the photographer) at the time, or just a few seconds before the picture was taken.

The vision also showed me that there were a great many scenes that were quite impossible to capture with a sketchbook alone. If it was the detail in a scene that was important, the artist could use his camera to record the instant, and later (in the warmth of his studio) compose his painting. For example, in the case of *The Ice Bear* composition: the bear of course would not pose for me – it had a higher priority being wild and free. And so the painting was composed of three main elements – the bear, the ice cave and the iceberg (three separate pictures – with some free drawing in the linking areas). The overall effect is the way I intended it should be with the 'stillness of the scene' and the balance of 'light and darkness'.

Finally the vision had shown me how I could go back over my entire polar career, and by selecting those moments that were memorable or historical, I could compose a picture to 'represent' each key event.

Hope Bay at the Time of Leaving (watercolour)

'If one looks carefully one can just make out the Hope Bay hut in this painting, which is painted here as I last saw it in 1958. It was spared the fate of the Reclus Hut (of being designated an "eyesore" and removed from its original site, which I talk of later). Actually it was sold to the Uruguayans for a few dollars, to be used by them as a summer base only.'

Sunrise in Smith Sound
(watercolour)

'My first watercolour painting was of Avatak, my main travelling companion and our neighbour during our time living with the Eskimos in Northwest Greenland in 1971–73. It was a scene that still moves me.

'I had been travelling with Avatak when the polar night ended. Our sledges had temporarily become separated and when I caught up with him, I witnessed something I have never seen again in all my subsequent visits to the Arctic. In the far distance, I saw him performing his own private greeting to the returning sun.

'For a few minutes, Avatak stood gazing at the sun as it slowly crept above the horizon. As its light flooded across the silvery plain, he pushed back the hood of his parka and bared his head. Throwing his hands high, he turned the palms outwards so that they were bathed in the brilliant red glow, before finally placing them on his head.

'Avatak did not know I was watching him. For a long time I did not move for fear of revealing my presence and so marring what was clearly a personal and spiritual moment. In that moving gesture, when he celebrated the end of the four long months of darkness, it was as though he and the sun were one in spirit – and its warmth and light gave him fresh hope and energy, just as surely as it infused new life into the Polar World.'

'For a few minutes, Avatak stood gazing at the sun as it slowly crept above the horizon. As its light flooded across the silvery plain, he pushed back the hood of his parka and bared his head. As he celebrated the end of the four long months of darkness, it was as though he and the sun were one in spirit – and its warmth and light gave him fresh hope and energy, just as surely as it infused new life into the Polar World.'

'It was the third painting I ever did and it was magical – it just came, without thinking. I hadn't put any conscious thought into the composition – probably because I was worried about the stream of water that was pouring through the roof of the tiny garden shed in which I was painting, and the possibility that it might splash onto the painting and destroy it, being a watercolour. But thankfully it didn't, and this has become one of my most popular pieces of work.'

The Ice Bear (watercolour)

'I think your watercolour is brilliant. How you do it I can't imagine – it is sheer genius.' HRH The Prince of Wales

'The Ice Bear was the third painting I ever did and it was magical – it just came, without thinking. I hadn't put any conscious thought into the composition – probably because I was worried about the stream of water that was pouring through the roof of the tiny garden shed in which I was painting, and the possibility that it might splash onto the painting and destroy it, being a watercolour. But thankfully it didn't, and this has become one of my most popular pieces of work.

'Almost all of my paintings are based on compositions; after all, if you want to paint a polar bear in front of an ice cave, for instance, he is not going to stand there long enough for you to do that, aside from which he would come and eat you up if you did. So, you have to do it from photographs, and from photographs of a bear taken from different times, and at different angles, so you can see how the bear and the light affect one another. Then you have to set him against a background from another picture, until it is all put together as a single composition. It is the composition that is the main element of the painting I think, rather that the individual aspects of it.

'So for instance this particular picture of The Ice Bear was made up of three different photographs. Putting these things together in a careful composition is vitally important, but it is the input of the artist that gives it the magic.'

Everest (oils)

'The Everest painting was an oil painting – the first serious oil painting I had worked on and it was commissioned by the famous mountaineer Reinhold Messner (the first man to climb all 14 of the 8,000-metre mountains in the world – including Mount Everest, which he climbed solo and without oxygen from the Tibet side in 1980). In his commissioning message he asked for two paintings: one that would honour Shackleton, and the other the two mountaineers, Mallory and Irvine (who were last seen at a height of 8,400 metres through a break in the cloud up near second step on the Northeast Ridge of Mount Everest – whether they were on their way up, or were returning from the summit, is still being debated by mountain historians even to this day).

'The problem with Reinhold's commission was that he gave me no idea of the size of the paintings he wanted, and so I asked him to be more specific. His reply came back with one word, repeated twice: "Big, BIG." I took the word to mean a width of 3 feet minimum; but he had not been specific on the subject of the two paintings and there had then followed a string of notes between us discussing the options, before settling for "the James Caird's landfall on South Georgia" and "Mount Everest from the base camp of the British Expedition of 1924". The latter was very familiar to Reinhold for his small party of four had built their main camp "exactly at the spot where the early British expeditions camped on the Rongbuk Glacier at a height of 5,000 metres. We have good drinking water, a little bit of green, and a flat place for the tents," he said, and they spent a few days there (a surprising admission for Reinhold who is notorious for being almost constantly on the move); but "after seven weeks at an altitude of more than 5,000 metres" he was now well acclimatized, and able to "run around the base camp as if I were at home."

'The painting I was being commissioned to work on would clearly require a meticulous attention to detail, since Reinhold knew every boulder and blade of grass within half a mile of that camp, and added to this there was also my anxiety of knowing that this was my first serious work in the medium of oils on canvas and, frankly, I hadn't (at that time) even a clue how to mix the paint, or in which hand to hold the brush!

'Furthermore, there was the question of colours: I was to work from a black and white photograph taken in 1924 (which I borrowed from the archives of the Royal Geographical Society, in London), and every colour print I had studied in books dealing with Mount Everest gave conflicting results, depending on the time of day the photo was taken, the season of the year and, of course, the film stock. So I was obliged to take a guess. I did, however, try to speed up the drying rate by using burnt sienna, which may have accounted for the warmth of the general earth tones.'

THE GRAHAM LAND PLATEAU

'The Graham Land Plateau is hidden by the surging cloud and blizzard that is raging up there.
From this peaceful spot we had to go up into that Hell, and be very careful not to fall off the edge,
which is about 6,000 ft above sea level.'

WALLY HERBERT, JULY 1968

THE TOTAL DISTANCE FROM HOPE BAY to Portal Point at the tip of the Reclus Peninsula is approximately 300 route miles: my task was to map this whole area (approximately 10,000 square miles in total, including the coastal region) during the two and a half years I was based at Hope Bay. But we had to spend the entire first year laying depots of food and fuel to support this one-way journey for we had no aircraft as they have today. Also our radio transmitters in those far off days were extremely unreliable, and we had no guns with which to kill seals for the dogs and ourselves.

We were in fact almost a throw-back to the days of Scott and Shackleton in terms of our equipment and experience. My training as a dog driver was in hauling the food and fuel on sledges up the hill to the Hope Bay hut from the coast, and from the rocks of View Point (where we had landed the hut supplies in the middle of my first night in Antarctica), to the site of our new refuge hut. This invaluable and memorable self-training was the first 300 miles of a career that has now covered a total of over 25,000 miles, and, for most of the first year, my travelling companion was the expedition's physician, Dr Hugh Simpson.

Our first real sledging trip together was the standard run – the one pioneered by Dr Gunnar Andersson and his two colleagues 53 years earlier, across the 'Bay of the Thousand Icebergs' (as they called it), and for us it was a heady

Dr Hugh Simpson (pencil & scalpel)

'Dr Hugh Simpson was the doctor at Hope Bay in 1955–58, and my first sledging partner. I went to Lapland and Spitsbergen with him and his wife Myrtle in 1960.'

experience to follow such famous footsteps. We had, of course, by then read Nordenskjöld's book *Antarctica* (which was in great demand from our library of polar literature on base), and naturally our curiosity was aroused to visit Nordenskjöld's old winter quarters at Snow Hill Island. That adventure, however, had to wait until a route to the Graham Land Plateau had been established, and food and fuel supplies laid. In the meantime, we had a hut to build at View Point from the supplies we had landed on the rocks of the headland, and this occupied four of us for several years.

Hard at Work

So with all of these distractions a full year went by before we could plan for our journey, by which time the annual supply ship had been and gone, and we had a new base leader and several new men on the base who were looking to us 'old hands' for advice.

I had been appointed by the outgoing base leader (Ron Worswick – a 6ft 8 in giant of a man with whom I had made several long journeys in our first year) as the leader of the View Point satellite station – and had taken the role very seriously indeed (inspired as I was by Nansen's belief that an explorer worthy of his salt was one that did more than his share). So I had looked around eagerly 'for things to do', and had found plenty to occupy my time. Some of these were

Nordenskjöld's Hut
(pen & ink)

'We did eventually get our chance to visit Otto Nordenskjöld's hut on Snow Hill Island, and this was how it looked in 1956 just before we set off on our journey along the plateau.'

not essential – others were truly laudable: for instance, I noticed on one of my long walks over to Depot Glacier a lateral moraine with some strange soil polygons on its surface, evidence of a retreating glacier. Being a surveyor, I decided to make a map of them – even though I had no idea what they really were, or of what use this map might prove to be. I put a small stone marked with a number in the centre of each polygon and plotted each one with a plane table, and was astonished to see the patterns they created – and even more astonished to be given some praise by Dr Fritz Koerner (a glaciologist) for having taken the trouble to map them.

In a similar situation over at View Point, out of curiosity I decided to record the break-up of the sea-ice. I found a brand new school exercise book in the hut that had about 150 pages, and traced off a map of the local area on to the facing page of each pair. Then each day (when the visibility was reasonable) I would take off and go for the hilltops where we had set up survey stations, and from two known points that were plotted on the maps I would take compass bearings of ice features, such as prominent icebergs or cracks in the sea-ice. Where the lines intersected, I had the feature fixed on the map. These maps I would then colour with different pencils, and on the day that the ice broke up and drifted out to sea I showed, for the first time to my astonished colleagues, the cinematic effect of the ice breaking up by flipping the pages with my thumb. The effect, although not scientific, was every bit as dramatic as the kids' game of home movies, and the exercise book ended up at the Scott Polar Research Institute in Cambridge.

Another pastime that engaged me was plotting on a map, covering an area of approximately 20,000 square miles (or all the sea areas within about 250 miles of Hope Bay), where every single iceberg was marked, and all the states of sea-ice were represented with a different colour. This piece of work ended up as part of someone's Ph.D.

But the most original of my self-inflicted projects and the one that caused me most pride was undoubtedly the tidal observations. These were partly with a view to giving the Captain of the *New John Biscoe* an idea of the state of the tide at View Point, and how much of an ice cliff he would find alongside our hut.

The ice cliffs, however, were the problem – they were about 20 feet at low water. So I had devised a special contraption like a trestle with a long arm reaching out. This extended over the sea, and from it hung a weighted tin can. A line ran out along this arm and hung vertically down to the sea, and by 'bouncing' the tin can on the surface of the water I could get a pretty good idea of how much line was let out – and of course there were markings on it to measure the length of the line. I did, in all, one lunar month of these observations – one every hour – and again plotted the results in a graph book.

The results were most impressive: I could predict the state of the tide to within a foot at any time within a period of five days either side of a date estimated for the arrival of the ship. I believe the captain was pleased. My companions, meanwhile, were totally unimpressed by all the effort, and only entered into the spirit of the enterprise when I launched the contraption into the sea at the end of the lunar month.

A Pioneering Journey

The Graham Land Plateau is hidden by the surging cloud and blizzard that is raging up there. From this peaceful spot we had to go up into that Hell, and be very careful not to fall off the edge, which is about 6,000 ft above sea level.

This journey – made by four men and two teams of dogs in fifty days – was a pioneering trip that has never been repeated. Our aim was to meet up with the three men who had spent several months trying to find a way up to the plateau from their tiny refuge hut at Portal Point. The problem was this: the Antarctic Peninsula is the dividing barrier between two different

My Team of Dogs, Antarctica 1961
(pencil & scalpel)

'Dog teams are now banned from Antarctica. We were lucky to experience the freedom of travelling through Antarctica with dogs – it seemed not only the most appropriate form of travel in this place, but also heightened our sense of achievement and adventure.'

W.H. '63

weather systems, the Bellingshausen and the Weddell, and where the two meet, cloud is created. From sea level the plateau seems to be almost continually covered in cloud, and with the plateau edge being a sheer drop of several thousands of feet, it was not a safe area along which to travel for 3 miles, let alone 300.

We passed the 'point of no return', and with our average falling to less than 2 miles a day we were becoming seriously worried. What's more, the plateau itself seemed to be shrinking – at one place it narrowed to nothing more than a sharp ridge between two separate plateaux, each at an altitude of 7,000 feet, with a safety margin of no more than 20 feet between the crevasses, marking the edge of a sheer drop of 1,500 feet on either side. The feature was dangerous to cross with dog teams – each dog has a mind of its own, and none of those canine minds seemed to be aware of the danger they were in while crossing that precariously icy ridge.

Seldom have I ever been so sharply aware of the narrow margin between safety and disaster as when we stood on the south side of that place we called

'A sketch of my three companions on the Graham Land Plateau reading a note that had been left for us in the cairn, to help guide us down the treacherous descent to Cape Reclus.'

the 'Catwalk', listening to the whine of the wind and watching the cloud surging over that route, which had now closed behind us. From here we had no choice but to continue, and finally we reached a point from where we could see down the Reclus Peninsula with Portal Point at its seaward tip, 7,000 feet below us and 14 miles away. At that magical place, a snowy petrel flew over us and we craned our necks to watch it circle, then a little farther, and with Mount Johnston in sight, we came upon a cairn that had been built by the three men from the Reclus Hut, the first definite indication that there was a way down to sea level.

Their ski tracks were still fresh in the snow, and their message, in its plastic bag, gave us a bearing by which to steer in order to reach their tent at 4,000 feet, where they would wait for us for two days. We had one day left before they would give up and start their journey home. I remember riding the sledge brake on that glorious descent, with the dogs galloping flat out along the trail. Their breath vapour, mixing with the loose snow they kicked up as it streamed towards us, was like steam from an engine as we raced into the cloud and tilted downhill. In a few

'My map of the Antarctic Peninsula showing the "Catwalk" and other features that we mapped and named in the area.'

In Amundsen's Footsteps
(watercolour)

'We finally reached a point on the plateau from where we could see down the Reclus Peninsula with Portal Point at its seaward tip, 7,000 feet below us and 14 miles away. The ski tracks of the three men from the Reclus hut were still fresh in the snow, and the message in its plastic bag gave us a bearing on which to steer by to reach their tent, where they said the would wait for two days. Coming down from the plateau along a trail one has not ascended is extremely hazardous – especially with dogs. Man-haulers seem to think it easy because one isn't pulling a sledge, but they do not understand how difficult it is to get dogs to think alike – and there was a 60-degree slope on that particular traverse. Small wonder it was named by us the "Deadly Traverse".'

seconds we tore through the cloud, and then, with breathtaking suddenness, we burst clear of our blindfold and the earth fell away from us 4,000 feet down to the sea far, far below. For a split second the ceiling of cloud was no more than an arm's length above us, and the compelling sensation to reach out and grab it welled up inside us. The dogs raced for their lives with the sledge bounding in pursuit, until we finally over-ran the tent.

It was a fantastic 16 miles down to the Reclus hut and the names we gave to the various obstacles on the route are an indication of the age we were at the time, and the virility of youth: the 'Horrendous Drop', the 'Deadly Traverse', and the 'Crushing Cwm'. So long, it seemed, had we been on the plateau where the wind and the ground drift were the only sounds and the horizon gave no relief to the eyes, that the coastline had become a new world of life and sounds, of sea and strange smells. But the high sea-level temperature had rotted the snow, and in it we floundered and sank to our thighs, our feet slopping in slush.

For a month all seven of us shared the cramped space of that little hut, waiting for the ship to pick us up. To feed the dogs we constructed a raft out of empty fuel drums and two sledges lashed together, and this we paddled out to sea to kill seals that were asleep on the drifting floes. Ourselves we fed on the penguins that had they been wiser would surely have given us a wider berth, and we baked cakes and bread in an oven made out of an old flour tin.

Eventually, on 28 December, the *John Biscoe* was spotted weaving her way towards us, and our lazy, happy life in that refuge hut came to an end in a flurry of excitement. The dogs were hoisted aboard and secured to the ship's rail, and very soon the Reclus Peninsula was lying astern. I chose to leave the ship in Montevideo and travel alone back to Britain through South America and the United States and Canada – a journey of 15,000 miles that took almost a full year to make.

I did not see the Reclus Peninsula again until 38 years later, by which time it looked as though it had seen a few hard winters – as indeed had I.

'Eventually, on 28 December, the John Biscoe was spotted weaving her way towards us, and our lazy, happy life in that refuge hut came to an end in a flurry of excitement.'

Reclus Hut (watercolour)

'For one month, all seven of us shared the cramped space of that little hut, waiting for the ship to pick us up.'

Rescue from Cape Reclus
(watercolour)

'This is a composite painting (using two black and white prints); it was a means of getting into the painting all the men who were there at the time we were "rescued" from Cape Reclus. The plateau in the distance is the one we travelled over and mapped – and is now named after myself.'

Portal Point, Last Visit
(oils)

'This was my last visit to the hut before it was dismantled (because it was an "eyesore") and moved back to Port Stanley. Yes, it was in a poor state of repair, but it was one of the most popular huts on the coastline to visit from the tourist's point of view, and was a valuable part of our history.'

Icebergs & Penguins
(watercolour)

'Penguins (the flightless black and white birds so beloved by the tourists and so "tasty" as far as the old explorers are concerned) doing their usual thing of hitching a ride on an iceberg.'

M/S *Explorer* in the Lemaire Channel
(watercolour)

'As an explorer I never got to see the Lemaire Channel – and many other beauty spots on the "tourist route". And so I sing the praises of the cruise ships for giving me the opportunity (as a guest lecturer on board the "little red ship", the M/S Explorer) to see these places and to visit such historic sites as Cape Wild (where Shackleton's men waited for the "boss" to return and rescue them).'

THE ARCTIC EXPERIENCE

*'A blue-grey fog was tumbling softly around a dead campfire when I awoke, cold and stiff, on
the morning of 18 June 1960, rolled out of my depression in the spongy tundra, launched
the canoe, and resumed my journey along the fjord.'*

WALLY HERBERT

SHORTLY AFTER RETURNING HOME from the Antarctic I made an escape in an old Austin van up the coast of Norway, deep into the heart of Lapland, then on from Tromso by ship to Spitsbergen. My companions on that my first Arctic trip were Dr Hugh Simpson, his wife Myrtle, and their three-month-old baby son, Robin. Hugh had been my sledging partner during our first year on the Antarctic Peninsula (in 1955–56), and was the leader of our Arctic Expedition in the summer of 1960. He was planning to conduct physiological experiments on us and on himself at our field camp in Spitsbergen – right on the edge of the Arctic Ocean, only 800 miles from the Pole.

I was, however, obliged to return to England ahead of my companions because I had been invited to join the New Zealand Antarctic Expedition as a surveyor, and had also agreed to make a trip to West Greenland to buy dogs from the native hunters and transport them to Scott Base in McMurdo Sound, Antarctica. The only way I could get to the mining town of Longyearbyen (where I was to catch the SS *Lyngen* that was due to sail on the morning of 19 June) was by canoe, and since the journey would take three days, I set off with four in hand.

A blue-grey fog was tumbling softly around a dead campfire when I awoke, cold and stiff, on the morning of 18 June 1960, rolled out of my depression in the spongy tundra, launched the canoe, and resumed my journey along the fjord. The past three days I had paddled 80 miles through breaking seas along a coastline aproned in scree and scarred by rushing melt streams; under towering, fluted cliffs and curtains of nesting birds; and through ice-choked waters fronting the Van Post and Tuna glaciers.

It was a race against time, an exhausting, lonely and hazardous trip, and by the evening of that final day, dead-tired and frozen through to the core, I had been relieved to come upon a cluster of derelict shacks and mine workings, 2 miles across the fjord from the main town of Longyearbyen. Moskushamn (so I had been told) had long been derelict and deserted, so I had elected to doss down in a sheltered nook and paddle the final 2 miles of my journey after I had rested. But no sooner had I landed than a wiry, strained-faced man appeared striding down to the water's edge. He greeted me in Norwegian 'English', helped me to lift the canoe up the beach, then invited me to follow him 'up the hill' to his place.

The Hunter of Moskushamn

We picked our way through the debris of broken-down buildings, rusted engines, and abandoned mine workings towards a warped three-storied warehouse. Most of its windows were shuttered and

Self-portrait in Furs (Full Face) (pencil & scalpel) [pages 54–55]

Dr Fridtjof Nansen at Cape Flora in Franz Josef Land (oils)

'This painting was based around one of the most poignant moments in Nansen's career. Nansen had abandoned his ship, the Fram, *15 months earlier in a gruelling attempt at the North Pole. Unsuccessful, and at the end of his reserves, he met Jackson outside Cape Flora. This painting captures him shortly after his arrival and before he had bathed and put on a fresh set of clothes – and this was the very last time in his life that he would be an explorer in his natural setting.'*

the groaning door flapped gently on its hinges. Inside the warehouse it was dark. Pit props supported a sagging ceiling. The whole building seemed to be listing, and the rotting staircase creaked as we climbed up to the attic. My host informed me that he was the only inhabitant of Moskushamn, a recluse (he admitted) who had spent several years on the north coast of Spitsbergen hunting polar bears. He was at that time gathering stores and equipment for another winter, and that squalid attic was his temporary retreat until autumn, when he would ship by sealing vessel up the coast, occupy his tiny hut, bait his traps, set his fixed guns and wait for the bears to come. He was a man with a stare in his eyes; a man who wintered alone by choice – a nocturnal man who awakened at sundown and prowled around in polar darkness.

Several hours passed before I felt at ease in his company, for he was surprisingly intense and, seemingly, a nervous man. We came from different worlds, he and I, and yet we talked away the hours of sleep while the wind moaned past the windows. We talked about his life as a hunter. We talked about polar bears, and about the Arctic Ocean and its currents that had carried driftwood from Siberia to the rocky coast outside of the cabin – and by the time the mining town, 2 miles away, was waking up to another day, Hilmer Noice had sown in my mind the seed of a truly great idea – I would make a journey across the North Pole following the drift of ice, which Nansen had attempted to do in his ship, the *Fram*, from Alaska to Spitsbergen.

Dr Fridtjof Nansen – Man of 'Vision'

The brilliant Norwegian explorer and scientist Fridtjof Nansen was undoubtedly one of the greatest explorers of all time, and one of the great heroic explorers, and with him I have always felt a great empathy of spirit through many coincidences of place and time in our endeavours. He was one of the truly outstanding figures of the 20th century – a man of formidable intellect and immense vision and courage; a writer, artist and philosopher; a

The *Fram* in Summer on the Arctic Ocean
(watercolour)

'The Fram *was provisioned for a drift of five years and had a library of 600 books and an electric organ, and yet of all the 13 men on board, Nansen (the man of vision and science) was the most restless. This was mainly because nothing changed with the scenery from day to day – the only real changes were from season to season. This was the main difference between Nansen's concept and mine. Nansen could do his science in a small and relatively comfortable ship; but his ship and the pack ice he was measuring were drifting at the same speed, whereas my three companions and I (with our four teams of dogs) were on the move for much of the time and seeing new ice every day.'*

scientist, scholar, mystic, and National Hero and, in his later life, a humanitarian, and Nobel Peace Prize laureate.

He was blessed, however, (as are all geniuses), with a heroic yet oddly flawed personality – at one moment original and inspiring, and at the next, full of self-doubt and foreboding. Of course, this self-doubt was not apparent during his first voyage to the Arctic – the whole experience was far too exciting. He had set out on this adventure a few weeks before his 21st birthday (much the same age I had been when I went to the Antarctic for the first time). Nansen had taken a five-month sabbatical from his studies at university to join the crew of a sealing vessel operating off the east coast of Greenland, and this clearly was an experience that had made a deep impression on the young man for, within a year, he was fired-up by a newspaper article announcing that Nordenskjöld had just returned from an expedition to the Greenland ice cap where he had penetrated farther inland than anyone else.

This news had awoken a deep longing in Nansen to make his mark in history as an explorer, but for a while at least he persisted with his scientific

work, and when he finally wrote up his research in German and English, it broke new ground and raised his scientific profile considerably. Indeed, Nansen was way ahead of his time in the presentation of his arguments and secured his rightful place among the pioneers of neurology. However, once his theses were complete, he was, at last, free to follow his other passion – to be first to cross the Greenland ice cap.

It was the tradition in those days to seek the advice of the respected pioneers: Captain Scott sought out the opinion of Nansen who was older and wiser (although Scott then totally ignored Nansen's advice to use dogs for his attempt at the South Pole). Likewise, Nordenskjöld (30 years Nansen's senior) happily took Nansen under his wing, and advised the younger man: 'That in polar expeditions as in war, in order to maintain the confidence of the men, a line of retreat is necessary' – in other words, the Greenland ice cap should be crossed only from west to east (or from the inhabited side to the uninhabited and desolate side). Nansen, however, took the bolder position, and went the opposite way. In effect, he chose to 'burn his bridges' and use the goal as their greater incentive – a philosophy of which I totally approve.

Nansen's team, which included Otto Sverdrup as well as two other Norwegians and two Lapps, literally 'sailed' across the ice cap; by lashing their sledges together and using a tarpaulin as a sail they 'flew over the waves and drifts of snow with a speed that almost took one's breath away'. When they reached the coast, however, after a journey of over 400 miles and having climbed to over 9,000 feet, the ship had left without them, and they were obliged to spend the winter of 1888–89 living among the Eskimos, making their return to Norway the following year, to a heroes' welcome.

For some time Nansen had been working on a plan inspired by a newspaper article he had read in 1884 that reported on a theory proposed by Professor Henrik Mohn at a meeting of the Norwegian Academy of Science. Mohn pointed out that relics from the *Jeanette*, which had been crushed in 1881 in the ice near the New Siberian Islands, had been found in Southwest Greenland – this was proof, as far as the professor was concerned, of a current that crossed the Arctic Basin. Nor was this the only evidence of a current that flowed across the Arctic Ocean, for there were plenty of other indications that this was so (driftwood that littered the beaches of Spitsbergen and the east coast of Greenland, for example; and an Eskimo's harpoon throwing-stick from Alaska that had ended up on a beach near Julianehab in Southwest Greenland).

Nansen's logical mind had concluded: 'that this drift might be enlisted in the service of exploration', provided that a special ship could be built that would withstand the pressure of the ice. So his plan was born – nine years after he had read the newspaper article, his specially designed ship, the *Fram* (meaning 'Forward') set sail, with 13 men and provisions on board for a drift of five years, to put the theory to the test.

The *Fram* performed perfectly, rising above ice floes that would have crushed any other ship, but as time went by it became fairly clear that the ship would miss the Pole by about 300 miles. And so, after an agony of craving action at almost any cost, the *Fram* became a prison for Nansen; he suffered the most crushing state of boredom, and yearned for his wife, Eva. Finally the

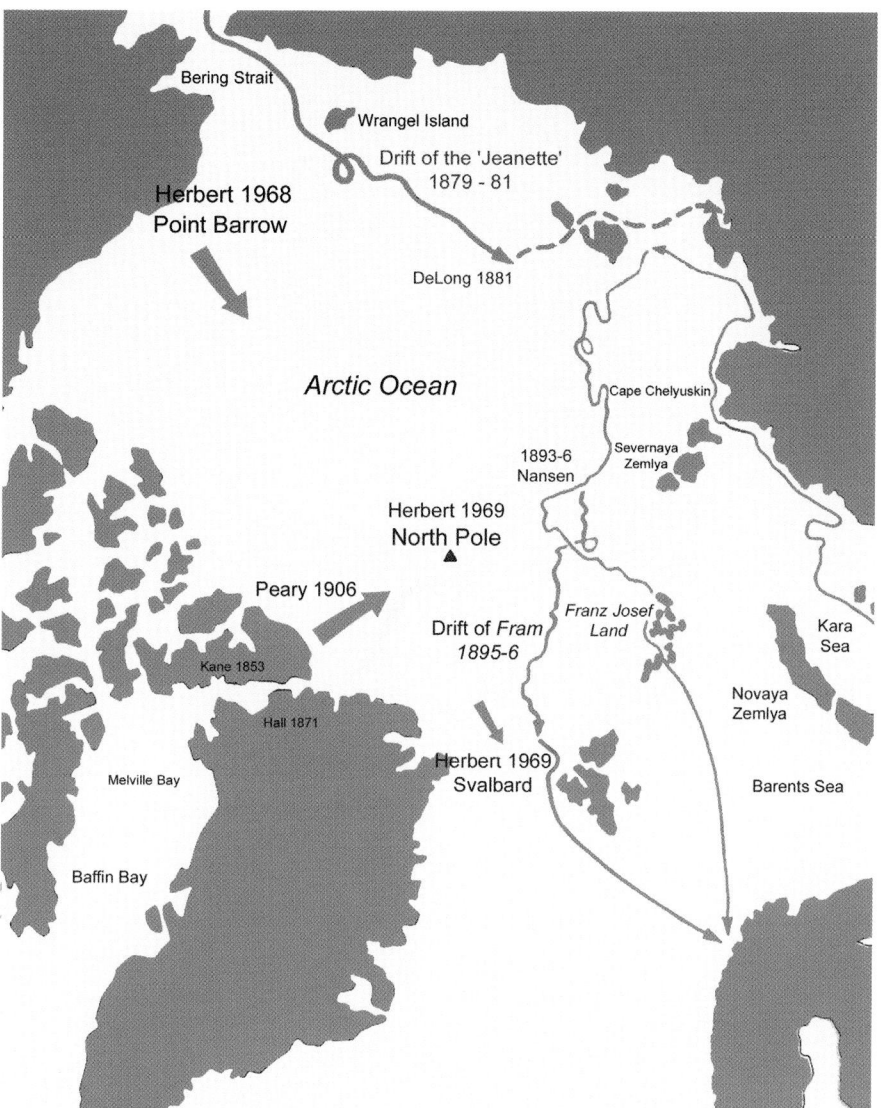

adventurer got the better of the scientist in Nansen, and he started to plan an escape from this confinement – leaving the *Fram* in the capable hands of Captain Sverdrup, he would set out with one companion (the stoker, Frederick Johansen), and with the dogs he had taken on board at Khabarova, he would travel north with food on his sledges for 100 days. This would give him the range of 50 days in which to reach the North Pole. From that point he would head for Franz Josef Land. There, he hoped, he would make contact with a whaler and take passage back to Norway.

Nansen was later criticized by Peary for abandoning his ship and crew – although, in fairness, it was the opinion of most of the crew that life aboard

would be less stressful under the leadership of Captain Sverdrup than it would be under the domineering influence of the leader of the expedition. They all, nevertheless, readily lent a hand to get Nansen and Johansen safely away on their journey, although they had no fewer than three false starts before they succeeded because of the many modifications and 'improvements' to their gear, and the ice conditions, which proved to be extremely hard going.

Nansen and Johansen finally got away from the *Fram* at latitude 84 degrees 4 minutes on 14 March, with three sledges and 28 dogs. Just under a month later they reached their Farthest North point at latitude 86 degrees 14 minutes north; however, aware of the drift of ice, they had no way of knowing the position of the ship. Franz Josef Land, some 400 miles to their southwest, was the nearest land that they reached after a hazardous journey of 130 days – more by chance than by good navigation for their chronometer watches had accidentally been allowed to run down and their longitude calculations were therefore out by several degrees.

Their troubles were less than over on reaching land, however, for they then had to somehow survive the winter and continue their journey the following summer without dogs – they had all been killed for food. Their only chance

of reaching civilization, some 600 miles westward towards Spitsbergen, was by sledge and kayak. There they might be lucky enough to meet a whaler and beg a passage home to Norway.

Nansen became world-renowned, and was given honours galore. He became an Ambassador for Norway, a humanitarian, and in later life was awarded the Nobel Peace Prize. But it was his Arctic achievements that were his greatest contribution to the history of mankind.

As a young man I had read with profound admiration, as so many other young men had done, Nansen's account of that 15-month journey from the *Fram* to the historic meeting with the English explorer Jackson on Franz Josef Land on 17 June 1896, and its epilogue of his reunion with the *Fram* a few days after his return to Norway. And even more intrigued did I become after completing our journey across the North Pole in 1969 to discover that at the very moment we reached land I had been the same age as Nansen when he met Jackson at Cape Flora. Naturally, when I was commissioned to do a portrait of the great man I chose to base it on the famous photograph of Nansen standing outside Jackson's hut on his skis (*see page 47*), a few moments after his arrival and before he had bathed and put on a fresh set of clothes –

for this was to be the very last time in his life that he would be an explorer in his natural setting.

These days, there is only the foundation of the hut remaining, but the backdrop of the little auk cliffs and their varying curtain of flight and sound is still there to give the portrait its presence.

Eight and a half years were to pass before the idea sewn by Hilmer Noice came back to me – a period of gestation almost exactly the same as that between Nansen's reading the newspaper report on the relics from the *Jeanette* that were found on the southwest coast of Greenland, and 24 June l893, when the *Fram* sailed from Christiania. This long gestation is often the case on expeditions such as these. In my own case, I was committed first to going to Greenland to buy dogs from the native hunters, then to transport them by ship and air down to Scott Base in Antarctica.

My task in the summer of l960 was to scour the west coast of Greenland for powerful dogs and, having found 12 suitable animals, to track down their owners and try to persuade them to sell. One of these owners and three of his dogs were different from all of the others and made a profound impression on me – this being my first experience of Greenland and my first encounter with a shaman. His story is very personal to me.

Meeting Innuteq

Innuteq was a Polar Eskimo who came from the Thule District of Northwest Greenland, and was renowned for being a breeder of dogs – indeed his whole team of dogs were the same colour (a sort of hot-ginger colouring, sometimes known in ladies' hair salons as 'red').

Innuteq really knew about breeding. In fact, he was a master of the art – and an art it truly was, for he was not satisfied simply with putting a chosen bitch with a particular male in order to create a litter of strong and intelligent offspring – whenever he got the chance, he deliberately introduced wolf blood into the pedigree. This was easy for him to do while he was in Northwest Greenland – he would simply make a detour when he was hunting polar bears on the coast of Ellesmere Island, and while over there in wolf territory, he would go inland to find a food trail then tether his bitch with enough seal meat to last six days. The combination of the smell of seal and the on-heat bitch would be enough to guarantee an outcome.

His aim, of course, was to produce the perfect litter and the time had drawn near to the fulfilment of his dream. The date was 27 November l960, and his bitch was having her pups; all of his children were standing in a circle watching and waiting for the pup with the desired colouring to be born, but it was the last of the litter to arrive and it was dead. All five of the others had been born alive but were the wrong colour. Innuteq had taken each one of

them outside, banged their head on the wooden step and tossed them onto the roof, so the children were very afraid and were utterly silent. Their father, being a shaman, tried various amulets and incantations to bring the last pup to life, but they hadn't worked, and he was embarrassed and annoyed that his children were watching. Finally he picked up the little pup and blew into its nose and mouth. Miraculously the little creature began to breathe, and its first breath was a shaman's breath. His children were delighted, and Innuteq had saved face.

The house of Innuteq was a shack – one of a small nest of shacks called Iglumiut on the coast one mile from the settlement of Jakobshavn. His dogs roamed free over a vast territory, for they had no boundary in any direction except for that imaginary line that, like a draw cord, held the settlement in place. Innuteq, as I later discovered, was born on 24 October l934 – the very same day as myself. However, there the similarity ended, for the place where Innuteq first saw the light of day (on 17 February l934 – the day the sun returned after the long polar night) was a hut called Neqe – at 78 degrees north latitude, the most northerly hunters' hut in the world.

Innuteq, as the youngest in a family of six, had been orphaned at one year of age and adopted by a dear old man named Odaq whose own father had been the legendary shaman Sorqaq. Sorqaq had been a great bear hunter – one of the greatest ever known among the Polar Eskimos. He had been famous too for his dogs – every one of which was black. Indeed, he was never known to have had a dog of any other colour – a fact that had made a strong impression on the boy Innuteq by its magical implication.

Odaq, in spite of his age, had also strongly influenced the boy during his formative years, so that by the time Innuteq was 12 he had already killed his first seal – an occasion that had been celebrated by both boy and man with the traditional Eskimo ritual of putting the bones of the seal back into the sea so that the animal would be reincarnated and return again to the hunter. But the proud old man had also on that occasion given Innuteq a present – his most treasured possession, an alarm clock (which did not work), and within a few days of that 'time mark' in the young hunter's life, he had had his first experience of magic.

It happened while he was out hunting hares, alone in the hills behind Neqe. At first he had assumed it was a man approaching, but it turned out to be an apparition – a friendly spirit who felt sorry for Innuteq because he was an orphan. Innuteq was, of course, very frightened, and ran home to tell Odaq what he had seen. To the boy's surprise, however, his story delighted the old man, for according to him, to have seen such a spirit was surely a sign that the boy would one day be a shaman. The old man had then told the young hunter about his own father, Sorqaq, and admitted that he himself had been a 'small'

King Dog (pencil & scalpel)

'King Dog was based on one of Innuteq's dogs that I bought from him and took down to the Antarctic in 1960 to be in my team for two consecutive summers' field work.'

shaman before the missionaries arrived. He, however, urged Innuteq to keep secret his relationship with his spirit 'helper' and all of the other things he had told the boy about the world of 'spirit', for he feared that Innuteq might be ridiculed by the Danes and the young 'educated' Greenlanders who lived in the Thule District.

Innuteq's 'helping spirit' appeared to him frequently over the years between the ages of 12 and 16, and during this period it became obvious to the old man that the boy was destined also to be a great hunter. But Innuteq was not a popular young man. In truth he was a loner who felt different from others because of the dark secret that he had been advised to keep. Unlike the others of his own age in the Thule District of Northwest Greenland, he had not been to school; had no desire to learn Danish; no respect for the white man, and no interest whatsoever in the outside world. The consuming passion of his life was hunting.

So, what was this pure-blooded Polar Eskimo doing in that nest of shacks at Iglumiut, a mile from the settlement of Jakobshavn – some 500 miles south of the place where he was born? The short answer is that in 1951 Odaq's wife had died, and the following year (at the age of 74) Odaq had also finally released his somewhat frail hold on life, so that by the time Innuteq was 18 years old he was completely alone. In that frame of mind, he had packed his bags with the few possessions that he had, loaded his sledge, and set out to travel as far away from the Thule District as his 'red' team of dogs would carry him.

Among those 'few possessions' was the alarm clock that the old man had given to Innuteq on the day he had killed his first seal. It had been given to the old man in exchange for a fine pair of walrus tusks by a sailor from one of the white man's ships many years earlier, and it had been the old man's pride and joy. For six years Innuteq had treasured it even though it did not work, and now he treasured it even more, for, in the last winter of the old man's life, Innuteq had taken the clock apart, discovered the principle upon which it worked and, to the old man's joy and amazement, the 18-year-old had repaired it.

The Last of My Dogs
(watercolour)

'I bought most of my dogs from hunters in Northwest Greenland for both my Arctic and Antarctic expeditions. These were semi-wild wolf-dogs that were bred to be hardy, working dogs.'

Since then the clock had worked after a fashion. It had ticked when it was wound up and its hands had moved around its face, and this, as far as Innuteq was concerned, was all that it was required to do. Never once had the alarm rung – it had merely given a metallic cough every time the small hand drew level with the figure 6. Since the young hunter did not need to know the time of day, he had allowed the clock the privilege of keeping time for its own sweet sake – so that even among clocks that kept poor time, this one was unique.

Yes, Innuteq was very 'different' from the other men around. Not only did he speak a different Greenlandic dialect, and come from a different culture, but he was also very eccentric – some would even say 'dangerous'.

Stories were told in whispered tones that: 'when he stalks, his body is transformed into a body like that of his prey', and that he 'keeps the company of seals, and lying with them, slits their throats'. Some even told me that 'it is the shaman's "spirit helpers" that stain the pelt of each pup red while still in the belly of his pregnant bitches'. The children of Innuteq must have been puzzled by stories as fanciful and 'wrong' as these, for with their own eyes they had sometimes seen their father's bitches give birth to pups that were not red

enough, and had seen those pups carried by him from the shack, then killed and tossed up on the roof.

Certainly Innuteq was a shaman, and a fearsome-looking one at that, for his face reflected the raw expression of his mind, and even his wife (I had the impression) was scared to look into his eyes. But I am inclined to think that he played on the fear he invoked in his neighbours simply to keep them safely at bay, for with myself (in my innocence) as the only exception, no one ever visited him, or even crossed into the territory of his amazing pack of dogs.

Needless to say, it was the story of this man and his dogs that led me, in 1966, to choose the Thule District as the one place in the whole of the Arctic that I had to visit in order to learn from the hunters how to drive dogs the Eskimo way, and how to live in their world.

But, in the meantime, I had to get the dogs I had collected along the coast safely down to Sondre Stromfjord, and then by plane via the USA, Hawaii, Fiji, and Christchurch, New Zealand, down to McMurdo Sound, in Antarctica, where I would be spending the next two years in the field making maps in the historic territory of Scott, Shackleton and Amundsen.

'In the past three days I had paddled 80 miles through breaking seas along a coastline aproned in scree and scarred by rushing melt stream; under towering, fluted cliffs and curtains of nesting birds.'

Self-portrait in Furs (Full Face) (pencil & scalpel)

'The original portrait on which this drawing was based was taken by Allan Gill up in North Greenland when we were attempting the circumnavigation of Greenland. I look much older than I do now because the ice wrinkles the skin.'

Wally Herbert 1991

'The Fram performed perfectly, rising above ice floes that would have crushed any other ship.'

The *Fram* in Winter on the Arctic Ocean (watercolour)

'Nansen was a visionary, and his ship the Fram is a perfect illustration of the way his mind worked. Nansen's logical mind had concluded: "that this drift [of ice across the Arctic Ocean] might be enlisted in the service of exploration" provided that a special ship could be built that would withstand the pressure of the ice. The Fram performed perfectly, rising above ice floes that would have crushed any other ship.'

Terra Nova Meets the *Fram* (watercolour)

'I had a black and white picture of the Terra Nova meeting the Fram at the Bay of Whales, with the Fram on the right and the Terra Nova coming in from the left-hand side. I liked the idea of slightly changing things in these historical pictures so that it is as if the painting was created at a different time from the photograph. To make my composition different from the original image, I put the sails up on the Terra Nova and set the Fram back, so that in effect the crew had had time to get the sails down before the painting was finished.'

THE HISTORIC SETTING

'There, in Shackleton's hut, it was easy to dream. Time was turned back half a century by the adventurous spirits in that place, and I was unashamedly in sympathy with them. I was more aware of the atmosphere there than in any other place I have visited.'

Wally Herbert

M Y RETURN TO THE ANTARCTIC was a totally different experience from my first voyage south in the old *John Biscoe*; for one thing it was a flight in a US Navy Globemaster packed to its limit with boxes of all sizes and shapes, and with 12 dog crates loaded on the platform that served as a lift (so that in the event of a disaster where some part of the load had to be jettisoned, the dogs would be given the lowest priority). And there would be just a few hours of flying time compared with several days of stormy seas crossing the Drake Passage. But the most stunning experience was flying over the Ross Sea, and seeing, far below, the unmistakable coastline of McMurdo Sound and the winter quarters of Scott and Shackleton, about which I had read with avid interest when I was at Hope Bay, but at that time had never dreamt I would get to see.

Landing on the ice runway at McMurdo Sound was a new experience for me. There was not a breath of wind, and the air was crystal clear and sharp. It was, however, quite unlike the Antarctic Peninsula; here there was grandeur – space for the mountains to grow to great heights and yet look small under the dome of cold blue sky. Mount Erebus, at 12,450 feet, was dwarfed by the immensity of the scene – and yet none of my fellow passengers on the aircraft wanted to join me in walking to the base known as McMurdo City, probably wisely, as there was low ground drift snaking across the ice by the time I staggered into the main American base, which housed as many as 600 men in the summer months.

After breakfast in the mess hall, I set off again to walk to Scott Base, and in my innocence asked directions from one of the Seebees. He admitted he was unsure – indeed, in truth, he had never heard of it – but eventually I made my own way there and found it to be a neat cluster of huts – resembling a centre trace dog team of yellow painted boxes on either side of a covered passageway. Scattered about were a few other huts that no doubt housed the scientific apparatus and the garages for the vehicles – two weasels, three Fergusson tractors and a retired Sno-cat that had made the Trans-Antarctic journey with Sir Vivian Fuchs in 1957. There was also a huge aircraft hanger, redundant except as a storage space for food.

The base had been built by the Ross Sea Party of the Commonwealth Trans-Antarctic Expedition in 1957 under the leadership of Sir Edmund Hillary, and had been occupied by the New Zealand parties ever since. In terms of efficiency, it was a brilliant design, but it was in my view soul-less and metallic – every door in the place had a 'fridge-type' sound and look about it, and opened into a resonant porch in which hung the anoraks and grubby outer clothing of those who had passed through another 'fridge door' to the inner mess room. The windows throughout the base were tiny and square-shaped – presumably to reduce the flow of warm air to the outside world (into which my colleagues rarely ventured for they were by and large scientists and sedentary; no doubt highly qualified, but totally lacking in enthusiasm for the Polar World). Only two of us out of the 12 men on base had any real interest in sledging and mapping, and we spent most of the time in the sledge-workshop and the adjoining survey den when we were not looking after the dogs.

The dogs, however, were kept outside (down on the ice shelf in front of the base) and they were there for the whole of the winter without exercising, so at the first opportunity to get out on a trip we gladly took it. We set off to visit the winter quarters of Shackleton and Scott.

Sir Ernest Shackleton – Charismatic Leader

Unlike Nansen, who had an aristocratic bearing and a daunting intellect, and who found close friendships with men uncomfortable – much preferring the companionship of women – Shackleton was of shorter stature, far more relaxed in the company of men, a man's man if ever there was one. His men referred to him as 'The Boss'. Nansen was known (out of earshot, of course) as 'Himself'– the inference quite obviously implying that he was far too overbearing and opinionated to be regarded as a normal human being. This to be fair was perfectly true. Of all the 13 men on board the *Fram* it was Nansen who found it the hardest to settle, for, in spite of having a well-stocked library of 600 books on board and an electric organ, he lacked intellectual stimulation and there was no one on board to challenge him. Although the living quarters of the *Fram* were small and moderately comfortable there was always a tension in the air when the leader was around. Not so in Shackleton's hut at Cape Royds. It was one of the friendliest huts I have ever seen in the Antarctic.

I visited it for the first time shortly after the return of the sun in 1961 with Peter Otway. Peter and I had spent the previous summer in the field, and the winter at New Zealand's Scott Base working on our maps and taking care of our dogs, and were now preparing for a season in the field mapping in the historic territory of the Beardmore and the Axel Heiberg glaciers – the routes taken by Shackleton, Scott and Amundsen. During the previous summer a party from the University of Wellington had come down to work on the historic huts in McMurdo Sound – to rid them of the ice that had engulfed them and generally put them back into good shape. So Peter and I had the privilege of being the first party to visit those huts since their work had been completed.

Sir Ernest Shackleton (oils)

'Shackleton was a charismatic leader, and a man who until a recent surge in popularity – due to the release of films and books of his extraordinary journeys – was not regarded to be as much of a polar legend as Scott. In fact, in my opinion, had it not been for Shackleton, Scott would not have reached the South Pole.'

We had approached the hut from the south in pitch darkness, and on reaching a snow bank had stopped and set up camp, not knowing where we were. I was up at the first light of dawn the next day, and discovered, looming not 20 yards from the lead dog of my team, Derrick Point, where Shackleton's party had hauled their stores up the ice cliffs from the sea ice on 10 February 1908. Excitedly I set off to find the hut.

I scrambled up a small ice foot – a miniature glacier split with crevasses and tumbled in blocks – and on to a hard snow col between two rocky hills, across a small frozen lake and there it was to my right: a neat, warm ochre, sun-soaked hut nestling in a dip, as snug a little hut as ever I have seen. It brought from me a gasp of joy. Behind it, rising above a rock ridge, the white cone of Mount Erebus cut a fine profile against a blue sky.

It was a small pocket of kindly feeling – a shell of timber with a few relics left to taint it with the odour of age, and yet I entered that hut as Herbert Ponting had done: 'with a feeling akin to awe'. It was from that little hut that Shackleton and his three companions of the Southern Party had set off for the South Pole on 29 October 1908. Four men and four ponies nine days later watched their support party 'dwindling to a speck in the north'. To the south lay almost four months of dire hunger and, as Amundsen said, 'the most brilliant incident in the history of Antarctic exploration'. They sledged to within 97 geographical miles of the South Pole – an advance of 353 geographical miles beyond Scott's farthest south record of 1902. They discovered and pioneered a route on the Beardmore Glacier and discovered nearly 500 miles of a new mountain range. The hut seemed too small to have housed such men.

Endurance Being Crushed in the Ice (watercolour)

'Endurance Being Crushed in the Ice, like many of my other paintings, was an expanded picture. In the original photograph Hurley had cumulous clouds, which just didn't fit; it was supposed to be a very serious and heroic shot where the ship was being crushed in the ice and the sky was all wrong! I put in heavy stratus clouds with light shining through them, and it transformed the picture. I also felt it necessary to create more space around the ship, and inserted a picture of Wild looking at the ship as it was going down, which was from a separate shot.

'In my painting Wild is the focus of an intersection between the spar of the ship and the dog team (both from different photographs). This triangle produced a strong focal point, and made it an interesting composition. This was all done subconsciously at the time, but at a subliminal level it works, and it becomes a painting that an artist has produced, not a photographer.'

Even Sir Raymond Priestley, who had been a member of Shackleton's expedition, was affected by the occult atmosphere of that place. He wrote in his diary when he visited the hut as a member of Scott's expedition in 1911: 'The whole place is very eerie, there is such a feeling of life about it. Not only do I feel it but the others do also. Last night after I turned in I could have sworn that I heard people shouting to each other. I thought that I had only got an attack of nerves but Campbell asked me if I heard any shouting, for he had certainly done so.'

That little hut was set in a delightful environment and all day we strolled around soaking in sunshine, aware of the impulsion that had driven the Pole-seekers to exercise hard where we lazily ambled. Was it any wonder that thoughts of them rekindled my idea of dog-sledging to the Pole at the end of the field season? There, in Shackleton's hut, it was easy to dream. Time was turned back half a century by the adventurous spirits that dwelt in that place, and I was unashamedly in sympathy with them. I was more aware of

atmosphere there than in any other place I have visited. It was for me a stimulating experience, although on another occasion it might not have been so, for it had caught me that day with a rising 'Pole fever'.

Shackleton felt deeply betrayed by Scott dating from the incident a couple of years earlier when the Southern Party of Scott, Wilson and Shackleton had reached the 'Farthest South' point of their journey. There they had camped, and on that exact spot at which my party had camped the year before in circumstances identical with Scott's party – in a blizzard with zero visibility; but in Scott's case he and Wilson had conspired to leave Shackleton to guard the camp while they walked on to see if they might get a better view into a new inlet, which they were proposing to name in honour of their 'weakened' colleague.

But according to Wilson: 'We were compelled to return when we had gone a mile or two as we were afraid of losing our camp, the weather was so thick.'

Their extra 2 miles, however, were southward (making a new 'Farthest South' record, beating Shackleton's by 2 nautical miles). I had made this discovery during the winter at Scott Base when I had been working on my maps of the previous season, and was amazed that Scott and Wilson had deliberately upstaged Shackleton in this way.

Shackleton had also come into direct conflict with his old commander over the idea of leading an expedition to McMurdo Sound – Scott's argument being, in effect, that Scott had the right to use the Discovery Quarters and Shackleton should leave the entire Ross Sea region to Scott. The great pity was that Shackleton reluctantly agreed to Scott's preposterous demands and this nearly scuppered the expedition for he was unable to find a safe landing site along the barrier's edge and had no choice but to return to McMurdo Sound.

Scott believed Shackleton had broken a promise, absurd though it was, and yet he himself had entered Shackleton's 'territory' between his own 'Farthest South' and Shackleton's – including the Beardmore Glacier and all the new country in between. In fact, had it not been for Shackleton, Scott in my view would not have reached the South Pole.

Captain Robert Falcon Scott

To winter in the Antarctic is to climb a hill in the dark: a long, hard struggle because the mind and body are unfamiliar with the experience. At the summit – midwinter's day – there is a feeling of elation, the climb up is momentarily forgotten in the intoxication that accompanies the shaking of hands and slapping of backs. For some men the descent to sunrise at the base of the hill is worse than the climb – for others the run down starts easily, a soothing rhythm, a delightfully carefree loping movement that gathers speed.

That delightful post-midwinter rhythm awakened the minds of men who had been dormant and insensitive during the darkening period. We were racing towards spring. The survey office and the sledge workshop came alive with atmosphere. The smell of wood and linseed oil, rope and canvas, dogs, dope, blubber, tobacco; the clutter of brightly painted boxes, half-built sledges, filed rations bulging in polythene bags; the classical symphonies on the tape recorder, the buzz of conversation, and the chatter of the sewing machine built up this atmosphere of urgency, of expectation. It was a pocket of the old expedition spirit. In the forefront of our minds were the men who had

***Discovery* in Winter Quarters** (watercolour)

wintered there before us – and no doubt Scott's men felt the same way we did all those many years ago.

The *Terra Nova* Expedition had spent their first winter at Scott's winter quarters of 1911, not far from our base. And at the time mark of midwinter there was a vociferous din and revelry as they started down towards spring. 'We are all adventurers here,' Scott said. 'Of hopeful signs for the future none are more remarkable than the health and spirit of our people. It would be impossible to imagine a more vigorous community and there does not seem to be a single weak spot in the twelve good men and true who are chosen for the Southern advance. All are now experienced sledge travellers knit together with a bond of friendship that has never been equalled under such circumstances.'

We saw our first glimpse of the sun on 3 September – five months after it had set behind Mount Erebus. The shadows of our sledges and straining dogs shot out like feelers over the snow. The wind of the gallop, the creak of the sledge timbers, the panting dogs and the trails of vapour were sensations of rebirth.

There were one or two grounded bergs near Cape Evans occupying roughly the same position that the 'castle berg' had in Scott's day and around these we ran the two teams like a thread, and burst clear. We drove the dogs above the tide crack and camped on a narrow ledge of snow about 60 yards from the hut. The evening was very still and the long shadows were shredding the scene in strips of light and shade. We moved about silently, but the dogs without reverence made their usual hungry sound until they were quietened with pemmican. All four of us kept glancing across to the hut throughout our camping ritual, but not until all was done did we stroll on to the sea-ice, along the beach and across firm, fresh, printless snow up to the door of that timber shrine.

Scott's Men and Dogs (watercolour)

'In Ponting's original photograph he had a blue sky (which of course turned black in his monotone photograph because he had a yellow filter); a clear blue sky is unnatural in the Antarctic and I wanted to create a different effect so I put in some heavy clouds, with light spilling over the clouds and over the men at the foot of the iceberg. This had the effect of completely transforming the composition of the picture. Had Ponting been in a position where he could have changed the sky I am convinced he would have done so.'

The hut like Cape Royds had been restored by a New Zealand party the previous summer under the leadership of Les Quartermain, an Antarctic historian who grew a grisly grey beard and inspired his six virile young helpers to toil for three weeks with pick and shovel to clear the hut of 250 cubic yards of ice. Relics embedded in the ice were thawed loose outside in the summer sunshine and taken back into the hut by Les after it had been tidied and the shelves and bunks had been shored up; then with his historical eye and a passion for relics, he had allocated each piece to its rightful place while his men spent a further two weeks weatherproofing the hut and tidying the environs. We were privileged to be the first to see that hut mantled in spring snow, lit by a low sun; a hut restored, standing as proudly as it had in its first spring 50 years before. Thanks to Les Quartermain and his men there had been space for the spirits of men who had lived there to move around, and everything was in its place for their 50th winter in that hut.

To the right, dark and dingy, was the kitchen, and it was open to view once our candles had been lit, for no wall separated it from the rest of the hut. We saw shelves loaded with old tins, cups on hooks, a cook's table scarred with the thudding meat axe, and a dirty stove cluttered with great pots and kettles stained with time and stews. We were in the 'men's quarters' – we thumped into their table, and the creak of the floorboards and leaping shadows brought the place alive with movement. It was cold and eerie, but we stayed close together and passed on to the 'wardroom', which was once separated from the 'mess-deck' by a wall of food cases through which a door-sized gap gave access. Chairs sat to attention at the big, bare, austere wardroom table.

Behind them the cubicles, ramshackle structures stained with blubber smoke, were cluttered with remnants of worn-out clothing, grimy and musty.

Herbert Ponting's darkroom, a squat black box, stood with its door ajar. It was choked with ice crystals, spear-racks of icicles, and shelves full of frosty bottles of chemicals. In the right-hand far corner of the old hut was the science lab; in the left-hand far corner we found Scott's cubicle, and as we sat on Wilson's bunk looking across the chart table we could clearly visualize Captain Scott writing his journal.

The marooned men were among them – the survivors of Shackleton's Ross Sea party. Traces of their struggle for survival were in every rag that lay about and the grime that impregnated every magazine and book, every home-made scrap of canvas clothing and the sandals soled with bits of wood. Their privations permeated the atmosphere of boisterous fun and serious debate of Scott's 'amiable argumentative' party who had wintered there a few years earlier, and as the darkness closed in and we stumbled towards the door it was as though we were pressing through a crowd of unseen people. We reached the door and drew a deep breath, turned and barred the door behind us and made our way silently back

'Farthest South' Campsite of Scott, Wilson & Shackleton 1902 (watercolour) [pages 70–71]

to the tents: frail, small, but friendly they seemed, and the roaring primus soon warmed our chilled bodies.

We all four gathered around in my tent that evening and as a breeze drummed the fabric and steam rose from the pot our conversation bounced merrily from one to the other. We reminisced on the winter we had just passed through and compared it to the winters of long ago. We dug up old stories freshened with the gaiety of a tent crammed with good friends – the first camp of spring. Only one man we wished could have been with us then – Les Quartermain, who had been in his element the previous summer, scratching and chipping his way towards the bunk of his boyhood hero Captain Robert Falcon Scott. Every half hour or so during every working

day one of his virile young helpers had let out a yell of excitement and slithered over to Les bearing a relic. We could picture the old man holding up the Tilley lamp, his eyes and grey beard gleaming in the lantern glow, as another piece of the puzzle was reverently placed on a pile of what looked suspiciously like junk to a less experienced eye. Many little jokes had been played on Les, and not a few arguments raged on the subject of Scott's immortality. But Les, in a philosophical and academic manner, had defended his hero until one day when a heartless blow was struck. It stopped poor Les in his tracks.

Bob Buckley had been working away in the corner that was known to be Scott's bunk, while Les was down the far end of the hut sorting out relics. After a few hours Buckley uncovered half of the bunk wall, exposing a few old bits of junk: a pipe, a small calendar, but nothing that had not been expected. An idea then came to Bob in a flash, and delving through a pile of 1909 magazines he found the photograph he was after: it was a fine picture of a buxom bathing beauty with a saucy smile and a theatrical background. With rusty drawing pins the picture was secured to Scott's bulkhead, then with a yelp of delight he shouted 'come and see what I've found'.

I doubt if ever before in the history of that hut had men run so fast towards Scott's bunk. They all gathered round jostling for position and gazed open-mouthed at the pin-up. A look of horror came over Les's face, while everyone else shook with laughter. At last with tears rolling down his cheeks, Bob managed an enormous wink and said: 'there you are Les – so Scott was human after all!'

We could have used Les as an intermediary that night for, as we sat chatting, the wind increased and the hiss of drift spinning past our tent foretold the coming of a blizzard. We had no reading material with us, but had

Terra Nova at the Ice Foot at Cape Evans (watercolour)

noticed in the hut the 1909 magazines that had been brought over from Shackleton's hut by the Scott men, so we drew lots to decide who would go and fetch them, and the unenviable mission fell to me.

It was a nasty night. The torch batteries were cold and the bulb gave only an orange glow. I felt my way along the coast and up to the hut where the drift was sweeping a scoop near the door. I entered the porch. The door to the main hut went off that porch and I stood on the threshold feeling cold, and fumbling for a match to light my way to the table where the candles lay. The whole hut softly creaked like a wooden ship labouring in a gentle swell and each spurt of a match gave that place a dim form before the light snuffed and I was plunged once again into darkness thick with unseen shapes.

Fifty years before, to the hour, the whole party had been there except for three men who had set off to lay a depot at Corner Camp. That night in the hut they had been working hard on the final preparations for their spring journeys: '… a very demon of unrest seems to stir them to effort, and there is now not a single man who is not striving his utmost …' The candle flame leapt and its glow penetrated the darkness. I shielded its glare with my hand and moved forward slowly. Shadows crept around the room, the pale light moved over sleeping-bags bulging on bunks, breathing it seemed, fusty with age.

I gathered up an armful of magazines, disturbing an odour that rose off them, and around the hut beyond the weak pool of light groans came like whispers of reproach. Two chairs had been moved – they relaxed at an angle compared with the rest, so I gave them a wide berth and brushed past two furry 'hands' dangling limply from the side of a bunk and stubbed my foot against something sitting on the floor. The shadows circled as I moved towards the door; they seemed to float just out of reach then creep up behind me and rest on my back. It was a thoroughly unpleasant experience, and yet the men were friendly enough, and our hearts were kindred – it was only the age we lived in that was different.

My sledging companions were amused when I told them of my experience, but the subject was dropped before I was provoked to challenge them to go and feel it for themselves. The next day a blizzard raged and the only sorties we made from our tents were to visit each other to exchange magazines. They were fascinating reading but the smell they gave off was repugnant, and early on the third morning we dutifully returned them and continued on our journey as soon as it was light.

Captain Roald Amundsen – 'Professional' Explorer

On 16 January 1962 – 50 years to the day after Captain Scott and his four companions learnt for the first time that they had been forestalled at the South Pole by Roald Amundsen's party – we made the first ascent of Mount Fridtjof Nansen. 'Great God! This is an awful place,' Scott wrote in his diary on 17 January 1912, 'and terrible enough for us to have laboured to it without the reward of priority.' Those immortal words were singing in my ears for the 17 hours we were on that 13,330-foot mountain, cringing in a stabbing wind, struggling to do our survey, stopping every few minutes to blow into our gloved hands and massage our stiff bodies. The misery and exhaustion we suffered dug deeply into our reserves, and the long, long trudge back down to camp almost claimed the four of us. It was less windy down below and the sun was soothing, but in spite of the risks of resting we were compelled to lie down every few yards.

The sledge flags drummed in a stiffening breeze from the south, while we assessed our chances of successfully descending Amundsen's route to the Pole on the Axel Heiberg Glacier. Mount Fridtjof Nansen in one way had been a good mountain to us, for from the eastern side of its massive dome we had been given a glimpse of part of Amundsen's route. The icefalls of the glacier we could not see but the top terrace and the run off at the bottom looked crevasse-free.

We scorned the radio message suggesting that we retreat to the Otway Massif, where we had been landed over ten weeks before, and drove our teams around to the head of the Axel Heiberg Glacier. The evening we reached that spot was glorious. The smooth, soft plateau sank gently towards the brink of a bowl of cloud. Two ice-caked mountains rose on either side, catching the sun on their slipping faces scarred with crevasses and gaping chasms. The air was very still. The omen was powerful. We switched off the radio and made ready to descend.

We had read passages to each other every night from Amundsen's book. We handled it

with reverence and I had reread until we knew by heart the account of his ascent and descent of that magnificent glacier. But we found many ambiguities, for the narrative of his journey had not been intended as a route guide for future travellers. He had taken only two photographs and neither photograph showed the icefalls. He had made no maps, left no route sketches. We had no choice but to rediscover a route down the Axel Heiberg.

We could only assume that the amount of ice flowing down the valley was the same as it was 50 years before. We could only assume that the crevasses and icefalls, although all different, would be cut in the same general pattern, for the bedrock over which the ice flowed could not have been eroded in a mere 50 years. We could only assume that his account was true until it was proved either grossly exaggerated or, what was more likely, very modest.

Undoubtedly, Amundsen's route up the Axel Heiberg Glacier had been a triumph of courage, experience and good sportsmanship. The object of his expedition was to beat Scott to the South Pole. On the face of it there was no reason why Amundsen should not have driven his dog teams directly from his base camp to the Beardmore Glacier – a route to the polar plateau already discovered and pioneered by Shackleton. There was no written rule forbidding Amundsen to use the Beardmore route. But the idea of using the same route as Scott scarcely occurred to him. In his book, Amundsen says: 'Scott had announced that he was going to take Shackleton's route, and that decided the matter. During our long stay at Framheim not one of us ever hinted at the possibility of such a course. Without discussion Scott's route was declared out of bounds.'

By sledging due south he ran the risk of finding his path barred by an unbroken chain of mountains, and since he had no ulterior scientific motive for his expedition, as had Scott, the success or failure of Amundsen's expedition depended on finding a new route to the polar plateau. This was the challenge

Portrait of Roald Amundsen (pencil & scalpel)

'Roald Amundsen was a man who looked upon exploration as a career. He was a professional explorer, who planned his expeditions more meticulously and logically than most of his peers.'

that Amundsen and his companions accepted, and by tackling the Axel Heiberg Glacier, which from every angle looks appalling as a sledging route, they proved themselves masters of their own fate.

The Beardmore Glacier, as seen from Mount Hope, had given Shackleton and his companions the opposite impression. It stretched out before them as a mighty highway to the Pole. The glacier was 140 miles long and its gradient was gentle, rising only to 7,800 feet at the plateau. Even its direction was favourable, for the first half of the climb lay due south and the second half lay south-west. But whereas it took Scott and his tough companions 14 days to man-haul their heavy sledges up this previously explored and relatively straightforward route to an altitude of 7,800 feet, Amundsen had taken only four days, including reconnoitring, to climb to an altitude of 10,600 feet. His achievement was even more remarkable because he took a short-cut through the mountains, climbing to 4,550 feet, and making two descents totalling 3,350 feet before he even got on to the Axel Heiberg Glacier. His total climb up the glacier amounted to 13,250 feet, and his total climbing from the time he left the ice shelf to the time he returned from the Pole was 19,590 feet, as against 11,470 feet climbed by Scott's party.

Amundsen's trip down the Axel Heiberg on his return from the Pole was so uneventful and straightforward that it barely gets a mention in his book, and yet by reading between the lines of this master of understatement I can see how breathtaking that trip down must have been. He covers the crux of the descent with no more words than these: 'On the ridge where the descent to the glacier began we halted to make our preparations. Brakes were put under the sledges, and our two ski-sticks were fastened together to make one strong one; we should have to be able to stop instantly if surprised by a

My Map of the Queen Maud Range, Antarctica

'The Axel Heiberg Glacier can be found towards the left-hand side of this map.'

crevasse as we were going. We ski-runners went in front. The going was ideal here on the steep slope, just enough loose snow to give one good steering on ski. We went whizzing down, and it was not many minutes before we were on the Heiberg Glacier. For the drivers it was not such plain sailing: they had to be extremely careful on the steep fall.'

It was an overcast day, oppressive with tension; shadowless; still. The brink of the first drop could not be seen, but we could feel it waiting to swallow us. Amundsen had called it the 'severe, steep slope' and I skied towards it to judge it for myself, while my companions sorted out the gear we would take down with us on our reconnaissance. We dared not commit ourselves to the glacier with our full loads as we might have met an impasse and had to return; nor could we risk an accident on the glacier, for we had not been given permission to attempt the descent. It had to be done in less than four days. We had no intention of taking the heavy radio, and four days off air was the mute clarion call for search and rescue to begin. A route had to be flagged through the icefalls and we had to be back on the plateau by 7.30pm on 24 January.

We fastened the Norwegian flag I had made out of bits of bunting and torn handkerchief to the front of the leading sledge, prepared the rope brakes, called to the dogs and lurched forward along my sledge tracks. We over-braked the sledges and descended in perfect control, not taking the slightest risk that would jeopardize our success. Ahead a ground mist lay thick and grey, with only the dazzling crown of Mount Don Pedro Christophersen piercing it. We felt squeezed by crumbled buttresses of ice, sun-soaked and shadow-smudged, that towered on either side.

We struggled through the deep snow of the top terrace, our shouts profaning the silence, our tracks scarring the soft field of snow. The tents went up on a shadowless ledge with mist swirling around us. Six inches of snow fell on our outward tracks. Time trickled away.

Two of our four-man team volunteered to make their way back, feeling their way to the polar plateau, leaving Vic McGregor and I the rest of the food. We skied off the ledge and down a thousand-foot drop onto a smooth table of snow that reached out towards the icefalls. At the corner of the table the ground fell away in a gaping precipice. Before us was such a scene of turbulence and chaos of ice that words were stifled by emotion – I had seen nothing to surpass the power, the beauty in that scene of turmoil. Into the cwm, walled by frowning rock and capped by mountains of sliding ice, fell thundering, grumbling avalanches, exploding snow in white cushions, curling, settling, staining the floor with debris. We stood transfixed and stared in horror at the lacerated wounds and torn white flesh of the glacier far below. The knives of nature had slashed that valley with such viciousness that mere man – so insignificant – could surely not creep through it. But Amundsen and his men had done so 50 years before.

Which way had they come? We studied the icefalls through the binoculars for almost an hour trying to imagine a route, but scale was impossible to judge – we were at least 2,000 feet above the chaotic ice that was the crux of Amundsen's route. We had no hope of finding a way, but in order to get some photographs among those spectacular icefalls, we set off and free-skied down a switchback fall on to the middle terrace. It looked stabbed and scratched with darkness filling the wounds to the brim with indigo blood. Roped together, we probed our way towards the head of the bottom icefall.

We swished over small ice bridges with yawning crevasses on one side and chasms on the other. We descended like chain shot on truant skiis, and in the cold grip of fear we hurtled towards the yawning mouth and came to a trembling stop on the tip of a chasm. We picked ourselves up and as we dusted off the snow we felt the leaping pride of having safely negotiated the crux of Amundsen's route.

At the bottom of the traverse our meandering course began. We went up and down and around the lips of monstrous pits and chasms until we came to a comparatively undisturbed tract of the glacier then in another region of awful pits. At 6.30am we were through the worst of the icefalls. Ahead we could see a clear route on to the main stream of the glacier. We stuck in a marker flag at the only spot near at hand where there would be enough room to span out two teams of dogs and erect a camp. We were 6,000 feet below our depot on the polar plateau.

On our way back up the icefalls we stuck in marker flags at every distinct change of direction, so that on the descent with the dog teams, should the weather be against us, we would be able to feel our way between the crevasses by taking a straight line route from one flag to the next.

The next day we sledged back to the top of the plateau with the good news for our companions that we had found a route; however, permission had to be granted for us to be able to descend, so that we might be picked up from the ice shelf. Surely, we thought, this permission would be given for there were no suitable landing sites on the polar plateau within 100 miles of our camp. All four of us were getting very tired, we were running low on food, the weather had been bad for weeks and the temperature had started its autumn plunge. By the time permission finally came the polar plateau had become an awful place. Our faces became sheets of ice, our hands and feet died as fatigue slowed our progress to a halt. Frozen fingers switched on the radio, disgust twisted our faces as we heard more excuses – 'they are still in conference'. Then we were given permission to go.

On 5 January we contacted the base with the news that we had safely descended the glacier. We were just a short distance from where Amundsen had camped after his descent, exactly 50 years earlier.

**'Farthest South' Campsite
of Scott, Wilson &
Shackleton 1902**
(watercolour)

*'This picture shows myself at
my "Farthest South"
campsite in 1961 – off Cape
Wilson at the mouth of the
Nimrod Glacier, setting up a
survey station (the last of the
season). During the winter at
Scott Base, while working on
the field notes from the
previous summer, I noticed
that the campsite was exactly
on the site of Scott, Wilson
and Shackleton's "Farthest
South".*

'There [Scott, Shackleton and
Wilson] had camped – and on that
exact spot my party had camped the
year before in circumstances identical
with Scott's party – in a blizzard
with zero visibility.'

Endurance in Winter
(watercolour)

'To bring in the historical aspect accurately in my paintings, I referred to old black and white images taken by photographers such as Hurley and Ponting. Bringing my own experiences to the paintings was crucial, as I didn't want to be accused of simply copying a picture.

'Hurley's picture of Shackleton's ship in the winter was cropped very tight; by expanding the picture in all directions I had room for an aurora and a moon, and could change the light and the emphasis in the painting. Hurley's picture had a dark sky, with the ship lit by a series of flashlights on the bowsprit. I took away the light in the immediate foreground so that it almost looked as if there was a super trouper lighting the ship from the heavens – a spotlight shining from God.'

Endurance in Pack Ice
(watercolour)

'The painting of Endurance in the pack ice of the Weddell Sea was inspired by Frank Hurley's black and white photograph. However, the man who commissioned the painting specifically asked that the ice should not look as 'lumpy' as the ice in the original photograph. So I went through my collection of slides and chose an image of myself looking towards the land (which was visible on the horizon for the first time in 16 months, after making the first ever surface crossing of the Arctic Ocean).

'This is a way of paying my respects to Shackleton and his men.'

Launching the *James Caird* No. 2 (watercolour)

'Both of the paintings on this page are of the James Caird being launched from Elephant Island based on a photograph by Hurley. In my painting (No. 2) I have allowed more space to the left so that the sun's position (behind the cloud) is visible. Aside from being more in keeping with the time of day the boat was launched, the composition looks better'

Launching the *James Caird* No. 1 (watercolour)

Wally Herbert 1998

Point Wild (Offshore) North Coast of Elephant Island (watercolour)

'This picture shows the coastline between Point Wild and the eastern end of Elephant Island – another depiction of Shackleton's great journey.'

Landfall of the *James Caird* on South Georgia
(watercolour)

'Landfall of the *James Caird* on South Georgia *is one of the paintings I did for Reinhold Messner. Like me, he was a great admirer of Shackleton and he wanted a painting of the* James Caird *approaching South Georgia.*

'*As the exhausted crew were approaching the land after a long and terrifying journey, they briefly saw a magnificent range of mountains through a break in the clouds – they were only three big waves from the shore, and they realized that they were in a very hazardous position: the shore was too hostile to land on, so they had to turn around and flee back out to sea and land a little farther down the coast. But that split in the clouds and waves gave Shackleton's men the first sight of land that they had had on that trip. I was able to find a picture taken from more or less the same position as Shackleton's* James Caird *and used that as a basis for my painting.*

'*In my composition the* James Caird *was in the foreground and the mountains in the background with a wild sea and sky. I was able to work out the angle of the sun above the horizon through the nautical almanac, which is very useful to me in all these situations; being a navigator I can calculate quite well where the sun should be.*

'*It was important to me to create the sense of drama in that moment, so the sea is wild: 40-foot waves, which are much higher than the highest point of the mast of the* James Caird. *I tried to capture the difference between the solidity of the magnificent mountains and the fast-running sea, so I made the sea a little bit blurred and the land solid.*'

***Terra Nova* in Ice 1910
(Based on Ponting)**
(watercolour)

Terra Nova in the Storm
(watercolour)

'Terra Nova in the Storm *was based on Ponting's famous picture of the storm the ship encountered going down to the Antarctic in 1910. The ship is keeling over and Ponting has it cropped in such a way that the ship fills most of the frame. As he had only a 50th of a second exposure the sea was blurred, so he cropped off the sea and left just the ship, with the men working the pumps on the flooded deck.*

'In the original photograph the rigging from the ship fell across the sea; then on the men's side the water from the previous wave was washing across the decks. It seemed to me that these elements were linked, and that appealed to me.

'I broke all the rules with that painting by drawing a diagonal from left-hand bottom to right-hand top and putting in the ship on one side and the sea on the other — expanding the frame so that more of the sea was seen, and then used a storm-whipped sea from another photograph to add drama. This was done without any conscious thought — the composition simply seemed to require it. But it also made the statement, with the rigging crossing over the sea, and the waves crashing on deck, that man is in harmony with the sea: despite the action in the picture, he is in harmony with the sea because he wouldn't survive without being in tune with it. With this diagonal, with man on the one side and the sea on the other, battling it out, they nevertheless have a balance between them.'

THE ARCTIC OCEAN

*'Man has crossed all the deserts, climbed the highest mountains, made his first cautious probes
into the oceans and into space and there is only one pioneer journey left to be made on the surface
of this planet – a journey across the top of the world.'*

WALLY HERBERT, JULY 1967

AS I WAITED DURING THOSE TWO LAZY DAYS for the aircraft to pick us up after our successful expedition through the Axel Heiberg, my thoughts turned north. There was nothing south of me, except the South Pole – which, prohibited to me, had lost its appeal. To the north lay my future, to the south my past.

I had dreamed up several exciting ideas for expeditions – such as the descent of the Blue Nile in Ethiopia with Sebastian Snow, the author and adventurer, and other adventures even more out of my normal field, but eventually I came to the conclusion that there was only one journey that would qualify as being described as my 'destiny' – namely the journey suggested by the reclusive old hunter in the derelict mine of Moskushamn on the night of l8 June l960.

On my return to England I began to plan a training programme in Greenland, and naturally my thoughts turned to those polar heroes who had gone before me, and in particular to Dr Frederick A Cook, who had claimed, as had Cdr Robert E. Peary, that he was the first man to reach the North Pole.

The Training Programme in Greenland

Dr Cook has been given a hard time by almost every writer with truly 'polar' credentials – that is to say, those very few writers who have actually been to the High Arctic and driven dogs across the polar pack. I wanted to know from my own experience how much of Cook's story of his 1908 North Pole journey was true (since at least part of it must be true because his winter 'den' on Devon Island has been found, and he returned to

Northwest Greenland in 1909 with the two Eskimos with whom he set out). So the obvious training ground for our own journey across the North Pole was to retrace Cook's route across Ellesmere Island to the shores of the Arctic Ocean; to pick up his homeward trail, and follow it south to Devon Island – a journey totalling 1,500 miles. Allan Gill and Roger Tufft were to join me on this expedition – Dr 'Fritz' Koerner, having recently got married, was otherwise engaged.

The Cook element in this motive for heading for Northwest Greenland, however, was only a part of the reason for this particular choice. At Hope Bay (where all three of us had been at one time or another) we had an exceptional library of polar books, and all three of us had read all the classics of exploration – Arctic and Antarctic – including those of every explorer who had travelled with the Polar Eskimos of Northwest Greenland, notably all the books by Peary, Sverdrup, Rasmussen, Freuchen and, of course, Dr Frederick Cook. But naturally we felt we had learned something about travelling with dogs in the Antarctic, and it had come as a shock to discover that we were raw beginners in the world of the Eskimos and that there was a lot we had to learn from them.

It was not until after four long months of polar darkness that we finally found a 'face-saving' ground, which could be regarded as a sort of compromise between the white man and the native hunter. This had taken the form of an arrangement with a brilliant young hunter named Peter Peary (the Eskimo grandson of Cdr Robert E. Peary, the American hero and Arctic explorer who claimed he had reached the North Pole on 6 April 1909); and a pure-blooded Polar Eskimo hunter, a character named Kaungnak. It was a mutually beneficial arrangement whereby we would travel with them and

Portrait of Dr Frederick Cook (pencil & scalpel)

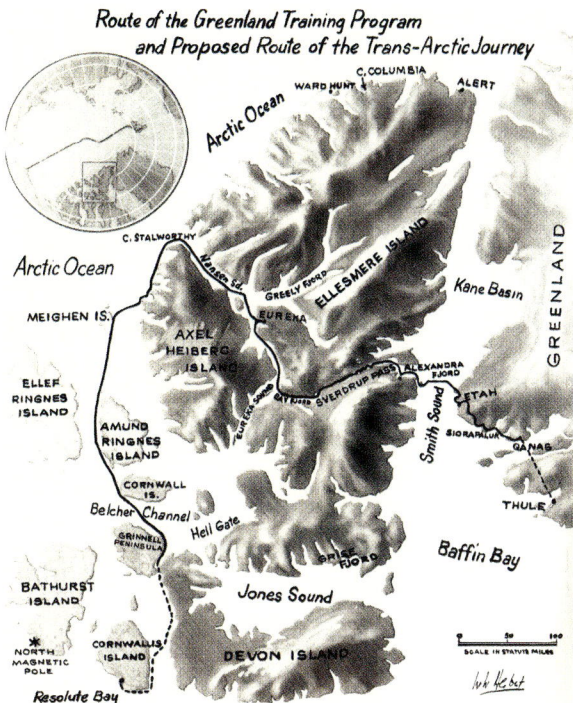

Map of Greenland Training Programme

'Setting out on 26 February 1967 after a winter spent in Northwest Greenland and accompanied by a party of four Eskimos for the first 200 miles, we travelled up the coast to Etah, then crossed Smith Sound to Canada. The Eskimos then went hunting polar bear in Baffin Bay while we three made a crossing of Ellesmere Island via the Sverdrup Pass. Our aim was to retrace the route of Dr Cook as far as the Arctic Ocean and to pick up his homeward trail somewhere off the northwest coast of Axel Heiberg Island – and this we did, although not without some difficulty.'

their wives for the first 200 miles of our gruelling journey – trading lightweight dog food, known as pemmican, in return for their guidance – a deal that I now shamefully admit sounds heavily weighted in our favour.

We set out on 26 February 1967, working our way up the coast to Etah then out across Smith Sound to Pim Island, where Sverdrup had wintered over in the *Fram* during his five-year expedition, and on to Alexandra Fjord – an abandoned Royal Canadian Mounted Police (RCMP) station. There our arrangement with the Eskimos had come to an end; but before parting they had each marked a cross on our map where they believed we would die.

The first of these crosses was a point about 20 miles from Alexandra Fjord, where there was a narrow strait with a strong sea current flowing under the ice. Here, they told us, the ice was dangerously thin. Well of course, when the Eskimos told us young men (who have just returned from sledging and mapping vast areas of the Antarctic) things like that we didn't take them seriously – we just assumed (foolishly) that they were trying once again to make the White Man feel inadequate. But sure enough at that place the dogs were actually putting their feet through the ice and pulling them out dripping with water – leaving a black hole in the ice (which on the surface looked perfectly safe). The last cross they had marked on the map was at the col midway across Ellesmere Island in what is known as the Sverdrup Pass.

The pass had been discovered by Otto Sverdrup on one of his journeys of exploration and had been retraced by Cook on his journey nine years later on his way (so he claims) to the North Pole. Since then only one party we know about had been on that route, a party from the RCMP. But none of the three previous parties had gone right into the canyon and followed its full length.

Sverdrup said of his discovery in 1899: 'The river fell in a steep frozen waterfall. We made an attempt to get down here, and crossed a large drift of snow into a fissure with perpendicular walls on both sides. The fissure became deeper and deeper the farther we went, and at last we saw nothing but a small strip of daylight above our heads, and all further progress west was cut off.'

We were to make the first traverse of that Canyon - and not out of choice, but because the alternative routes across Ellesmere Island that year were even

The Canyon, During the Crossing of Ellesmere Island (watercolour)

'The most difficult part of the crossing of Ellesmere Island is undoubtedly the Sverdrup Pass, which most years within living memory (and we spoke to many Eskimo hunters on this subject) has been bare of snow. In fact, the only snow cover to be found is at the bottom of a canyon, which, in places, is only a few feet wide. The painting I made of this canyon shows Roger Tufft standing on top of one of the frozen waterfalls – the dogs we simply let off to find their own way while we back-packed the loads.'

worse; so long did that stage of our journey take that we ran completely out of food and had to kill some of our dogs to feed the others – and we had to eat dog ourselves. It was, without any doubt, the most difficult part of my polar career up to that point and we were able to make it only by manhandling each sledge in relays between the three of us and releasing all of the dogs to wander through the canyon at their own pace. In the end we gave up trying to handle the sledge carefully and, after taking the handlebars off each sledge, we just pushed them headlong over the frozen waterfalls and slid down them on our behinds.

Eventually the canyon widened into a frozen lake that both Sverdrup and Cook had crossed many years before. There had been quite a bit of glacial retreat over the years – indeed, where Sverdrup had found that a glacier had completely blocked the flow of the lake, we found we could just squeeze by. From here Cook had sledged down a 'highway of ice' that he had called the Greely River. He wrote of that day 59 years earlier: 'the temperature was -78 degrees F, but the day was beautiful, and for the first time I felt the heat from the sun through the thick fur.' He was eating very well from the gun and how we envied him his sense of well-being and his romp along that 'highway of ice', which we found to be a braided stream covered in a sheet of ice that we descended by sliding helplessly from one rocky patch to another.

On the whole, Cook had described what he saw well (and likewise we did too), making allowances for his style of writing. Even the mountain, Svartevoeg, which Cook said was at the northernmost point of Axel Heiberg, we found to be more or less where he said it was – although several Eskimos had told us that he and his party had turned south and headed directly for Devon Island as soon as they had crossed Ellesmere Island. But it's fair to say we know that he and his two Eskimo companions had wintered on the north coast of Devon Island (I have actually sat in his stone den and handled the many bones that are lying around in silent tribute to their hunting skills).

And by all accounts, the Eskimos liked him. It was certainly a privilege to follow his trail for at least a part of his journey.

First Surface Crossing of the Arctic Ocean

Through the ordeal and sheer misery of our training journey we learnt a great many things about ourselves (and about the others who had gone before us – such as Dr Cook). A short, pleasant trip would have discovered nothing.

It had to be hard, neck or nothing: a gamble where everything was at stake, for if there was a weakness that this training journey did not uncover, the Trans-Arctic Expedition would certainly find it. The journey, however, had convinced Roger that the whole concept of the plan was weak, and so he had pulled out. Allan, on the other hand, had simply said with a nod: 'See you in September.'

I had arrived back in London on 30 June 1967, and had, effectively, less than six months in which to launch the expedition. Although we had literary contracts that were expected to yield £48,000, only £8,000 of this had been received, and £7,000 of that had already been spent. I needed a bank account, an office, a personal assistant, a car, and a bridging loan of £50,000. But the banks were being squeezed hard and armies of accountants surrounded the rich to keep the beggars at bay. Nor could there be any question of seeking royal patronage until our financial situation became a little clearer, and, to top it all, I was then informed by the Royal Geographical Society (RGS) that their support for the expedition covered only the Greenland training programme, and that I would have to submit another proposal and present myself once again for questioning.

Fortunately, by this time I had the support of a Committee of Management, their function being 'to … guide, council, encourage, temper my enthusiasm', and to use their far-ranging influence in the City to ease my workload, as well as to check (at

Portrait of Sir Vivian Fuchs (pencil & scalpel)

our fortnightly meetings in the office of Sir Vivian Fuchs) the progress of a project that I had been planning for four years on my own, and which was now building upon the foundation of their wide and varied experience. It was absolutely my idea, and yet I never felt at ease in their company – probably because they were all (with one exception) old enough to be my father, and because I had an instinctive respect for age, wisdom, and rank.

My Committee of Management were certainly rich in all three of these seemingly God-given virtues, and very shortly after they had all come together, we were blessed with the full support of the RGS, the patronage of HRH The Duke of Edinburgh, and the vice-patronage of two doyens of polar exploration: Sir Raymond Priestley, who had been a geologist with Shackleton and Scott, and The Rt Rev. Launcelot Fleming, Bishop of

Norwich, who had been the geologist on the *Penola* expedition of 1934–37; this was the last expedition to venture to the Antarctic entirely under sail, and the same expedition on which the bosun had been Norman Gurney (the curate at the church where I had been a choirboy).

I also found myself a formidably protective personal assistant (Frankie Ryan) – a stunning young lady with whom I would play tennis every morning before breakfast – a fast car (a perk I felt I deserved after my years of roughing-it in the Antarctic), and a bed-sit in London (the very same room, by a strange twist of fate, was used as a 'pad' by Sir Vivian Fuchs during his last few months in London before setting off on his historic crossing of the Antarctic Continent in 1957).

It was an exhausting time for all of us at the expedition's office, but, suffice to say, we finally raised sufficient funds, ordered and shipped 70,000 lbs of equipment to the two staging depots in the Arctic, and transported 40 huskies from Northwest Greenland to Barrow, Alaska, all within the space of a few frantic months.

The logistics support, so vital to the expedition, had been promised by the Canadian Forces and the Naval Arctic Research Laboratory at Point Barrow, and all the airdrops had been carefully scheduled. The Royal Air Force had flown all the expedition's equipment to the two Arctic staging depots, where the gear for each of the seven drops had been carefully labelled, weighed and stored. The hut in which we had spent the winter in Greenland had been flown to Resolute Bay, where it was to be kept until it was needed by us in the middle of the Arctic Ocean, and the Royal Navy had agreed to schedule HMS *Endurance* for standby duty in Spitsbergen waters to cover the closing stages of our journey in June 1969.

The Expedition Party

Dr 'Fritz' Koerner had been the first person I had invited to join the expedition. He had been a glaciologist with the Hope Bay incoming 'relief party', and we had struck up a friendship because of our common enthusiasm for field work. We differed in the 'degree' of our understanding of the polar world – mine being vary amateurish compared to Fritz's more academic interest in snow and ice. But what had impressed me about Fritz on first meeting him was the Nansen-like quality that set him apart from most of his scientific colleagues – that rare combination of a brilliant scientific mind and a 'spirit of adventure'.

It was some six years before we met again, by which time I had spent the summer in Spitsbergen, on the west coast of Greenland and in the south for two more years with the New Zealand Antarctic Expedition; meanwhile Fritz had been pursuing his career as a glaciologist both in the Arctic and the Antarctic. By then I had been working for several months on the general idea of attempting a surface crossing of the Arctic Ocean by its longest axis – a journey of 3,800 route miles that would take four men and four teams of dogs 16 months to complete. At that time no one had ever attempted a journey such as this (and even to this day, no one has ever repeated it) – and there was still a heated controversy raging between the supporters of Cdr Robert E. Peary and those of Dr Frederick A. Cook as to which of these two (if indeed either) had reached the North Pole.

Polar Bear on Pack Ice – Detail (watercolour)

Fritz came up with a scientific plan inspired by Nansen, although Fritz would not be stuck in the ice as the *Fram* was, and so would be able to measure a wider range of ice conditions throughout the seasons. Consequently his work provided the scientific community with the baseline against which all the measurements these days are made when discussing the rate of ice decrease on the Arctic Ocean as a result of global warming. During those 16 months on the Arctic Ocean he counted and measured 21,000 pressure ridges, and bored over 200 holes through the pack ice as part of his study, covering areas of the Arctic Ocean never visited before or since. Besides these glaciological studies and sea ice studies he conducted a geophysical programme of auroral observations that he made during the long polar night, as an air-sampling programme that collected particle fallout in this remote area – some of lunar origin.

The other three in the party each had their own roles: Allan was in charge of navigation; Captain Ken Hedges as the expedition physician took care of the medical and psychological research programme; and I took care of logistics and the radio.

Of course there were many concerns we had to consider when planning the journey: would the dogs last the distance? How well would we ourselves cope with the sheer monotony and the continual, crippling physical toil of a 16-month journey? Ahead lay a journey that no one before had ever attempted. It was to be four times as long as the ordeal of our training expedition the previous spring, and six times as long as an Antarctic sledging season. I made provision for each man at all times to have his own team of dogs, with eight spare sledges to be held in reserve at Barrow and Resolute Bay. In this way each man would have pride in his team and friction would be kept to a minimum. We would meet up with each other only during the day when we encountered some obstacle to our progress and would therefore look forward to the company of our tent companions at the end of each day's toil.

For convenience I had adopted the time-honoured arrangement of two men to a tent, but had taken the precaution of arranging for a changeover of tent companions at the end of each 20-day period so that we could avoid the 'two-tent splits' so common on Antarctic expeditions. I had even arranged that we should carry only three rifles – the idea being that if we were visited by a polar bear, one man (the one without a rifle) would be more inclined to pick up a camera!

Setting Out

Finally, Allan and Ken left London on 12 December bound for the Thule District of Northwest Greenland, where they would collect the 40 dogs we needed and, shortly after Christmas, fly on to our rendezvous point at Barrow, Alaska.

The last three weeks at Barrow before we set out on our epic journey were the most testing days of my life. For Fritz and his heavily pregnant wife Anna in Columbus, Ohio, those same three weeks were also a period of anxiety and great emotional stress. They were pestered by reporters, sick humourists, and

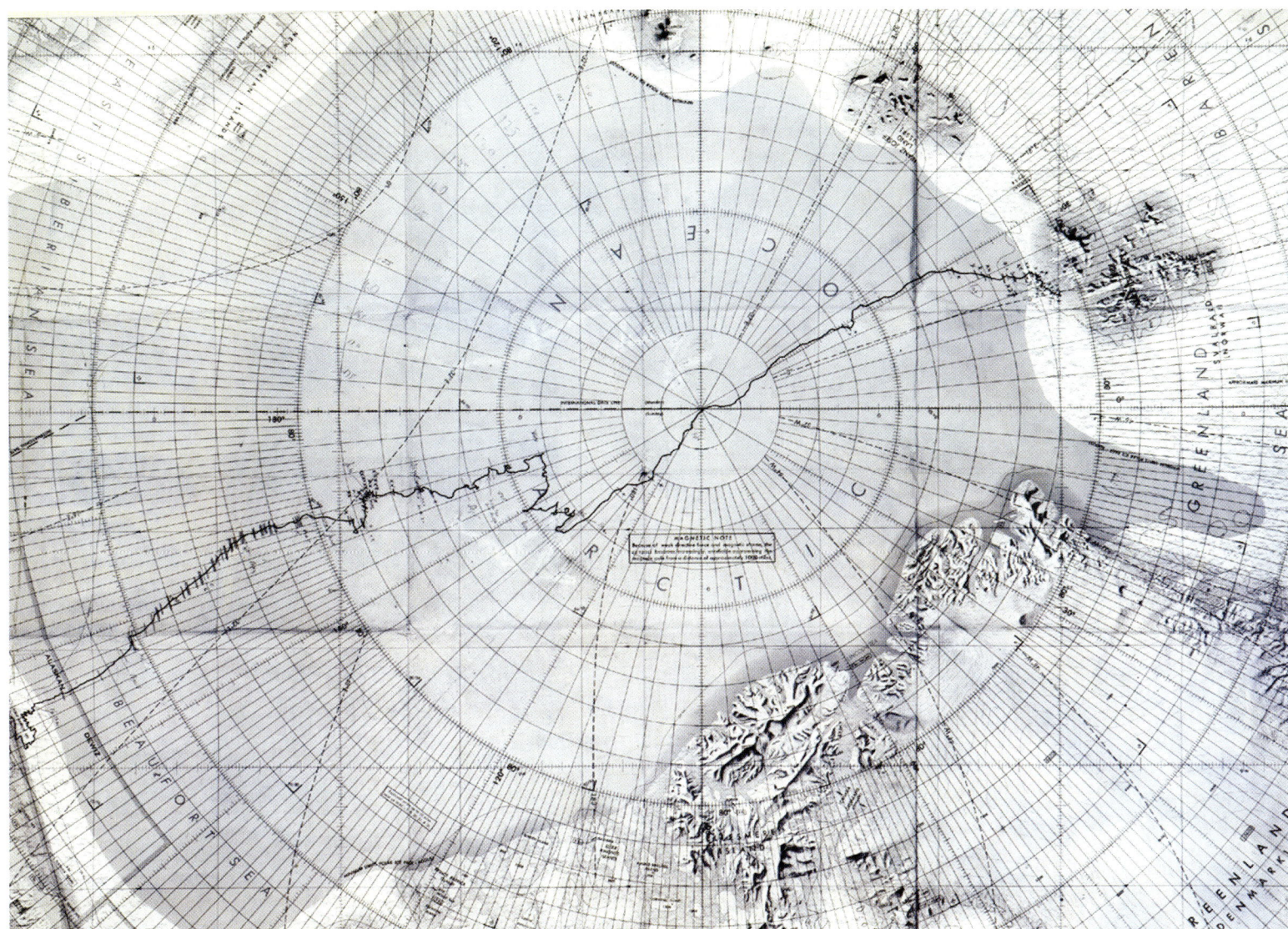

cranks who would telephone them at any hour of the day or night simply to condemn them for considering such an expedition – then, on 31 January, Anna gave birth to a girl; two days later Fritz joined us for the final few days of nervous anticipation.

On 20 February 1968: 'I signalled the pilot of the *Dakota* with a nod.' Our mission was to find a way onto the drifting pack ice, and our position at that time was about 80 miles ENE of Barrow. He eased the plane into a turn and took one last look to the north. The vast expanse of drifting ice was awesome – limitless. To the south, weak rays of sunlight pierced the clouds and scattered the ice with patches of light. Cracks and open leads caught the sun like molten silver and darted around on the surface of the pack ice before turning into jet black scars that marked the blue-grey skin of the frozen sea. It was a moment of profound relief – the moment of decision. Tomorrow, four men and four teams of dogs would set out on a journey from which there could be no turning back.

Our proposed journey along the longest axis of the Arctic Ocean would be a pioneering journey – a horizontal Everest that would mark each one of us for life. Our beds, most nights, would be on ice no more than 2 meters thick (and often very much thinner), ice that might at any time split or start to pressure. There would not be a day during the next 16 months when the

Setting Out from Alaska, 21 February 1968 (oils)

'This painting was based on part of the 16mm film we made of our journey.'

floes over which we were travelling, or sleeping off our fatigue, would not be drifting with the currents or driven by the winds. There would be no end to the movement; no rest, no landfall, no sense of achievement, no peace of mind, until we reached Spitsbergen. Most importantly: there was no possibility whatsoever of rescue.

By midnight on the eve of our departure the pace of preparation had slackened, and on that day I received a parcel from home containing the Union Jack and a note from my father that simply read: 'you forgot your flag – good luck'. I was so touched by this correction that I took it on the journey.

That last night at Barrow I remember very well: it felt like the eve of a battle – still, clear, cold, silent, with no one sleeping; an atmosphere heavy with private thoughts. I felt as though I was in a trench in the First World War along with the others – we fixed our bayonets and just waited for the

first weak light of dawn and for the young lieutenant to blow his whistle, whereupon, almost numb, we would all scramble out to face out fate. I was physically sick with fear, and the weight of the trust that my three companions had in me. Which of these two was the greater, I still do not know – even to this day.

I unlatched the huge doors of the warehouse and spread them open. The night was almost over. It was calm, clear, and very cold. The sledge moved over the floor on rollers, bit the snow, and slid forward, out into a deserted street smoke-grey in seeping twilight. I left it facing northeast at the end of two rows of day-bleached lights that pointed a perspective arrow southwest down the main street. There was not a breath of wind to dissipate the plumes of vapour that hung over each box-like building – the camp was still and sleeping and the only sound was of the throbbing warmth within each manmade shelter.

And so the scene was set at Point Barrow, Alaska, on 21 February 1968 for the final farewells, and the start of what most historians now regard as the 'last of the great pioneering journeys made on the face of the Earth'. It was an achievement hailed by the then-Prime Minister, Harold Wilson, as a 'feat of endurance and courage which ranks with any in polar history'; and by HRH Prince Philip (the Expedition's Patron) as 'an achievement which ranks among the greatest triumphs of human skill and endurance'. The full historical significance of that expedition is, however, only now, coming into sharper focus.

During the first few weeks of the journey we were in constant danger of foundering – and it was at times pretty scary moving over fractured ice, sometimes by the light of the aurora, sometimes in moonlight, but most of the time in pitch darkness. We were, however, too preoccupied with what we were doing to be amused or irritated by the odds of four-to-one against our success, which were being offered in the bars in Fairbanks.

The Challenge of the Ice

We were using techniques of travel regarded as obsolete by all but a few Polar Eskimos, in an environment that even to them is completely unknown. We hacked our way north from winter into early summer across the Pacific Gyra, where no one had been before – and no one has been since; across vast areas of ice barely thick enough to support the weight of a sledge, and at other times, across icescapes so chaotic and yet sometimes so tranquil, so deceptively still, it was hard to believe that the mountains of ice were no more than 10 metres high and the sea beneath our feet 3,000 metres deep. Our sledges were converted into boats in order to cross the leads, but by 4 July the floes were flooded with water and we could go no further. The Royal Canadian Air Force flew out our summer supply drop and we set up camp on a hummock.

The large, shapeless shelter we had built out of parachutes during the summer was, by the beginning of September, casting long shadows over a surface no longer familiar, for the first snows of winter had settled on our camp and had transformed the scene into a dazzling wilderness. But we could not stay there. We had to find another floe on which to set up our winter quarters before the onset of the long polar night, for the floe on which we had spent the summer was too far east to pick up the transpolar drift stream that would carry us as planned towards the Pole.

We abandoned our summer camp on 4 September and set out with heavily loaded sledges. Four days later we suffered the biggest setback of the whole journey: Allan Gill, when running beside his sledge, stumbled and fell. His injury proved to be a slipped disc. We now had no choice but to return to our summer base for it was the only sizeable floe we had seen in the area.

With Allan's injury there came an end to our hopes of correcting our course and getting ourselves to a position from where we would benefit from the favourable drift of the transpolar stream. Here we were in the middle of the Arctic Ocean, as the sun was setting at the start of a winter of five months of darkness, on ice that was drifting about 3 miles a day and constantly fracturing, opening into 'smoking' leads, or building into great walls of pressure. There is no surface on the face of the Earth more unstable than the drifting pack ice, nor any place more desolate and hazardous than a camp at latitude 85 north at the start of the long polar night (*see page 90*).

It was at that latitude 85, just as the sun was setting, that we received our massive winter supply drop of 28 tons of food, fuel and equipment, including the same prefabricated hut that we had used in Northwest Greenland in 1967–68 (it was really a padded tent, 16 feet square, with a kerosene-burning stove in the middle – and a warm, cosy winter quarters it proved to be). There was of course enough food and fuel to take us right through the five months of winter darkness with ample reserve for the following spring's sledging; but this precious supply had to be laid out in depots all around the floe in case the floe cracked up – which sure enough it did some three weeks into the winter.

The floe was by then about a mile in diameter and was surrounded by smaller floes over a total area of about 7 square miles. Then the floe began to break up. The nearest fracture to appear cut through the camp only 8 yards from a team of dogs and separated us from two of our five depots of supplies. We were obliged to dismantle our hut in a hurry, to shift all 28 tons of food, fuel and equipment, including all of the furniture we had made out of various packing crates and odd bits of wood, some 3 miles to a safer place.

One of the items that went on that move (where each object was worth its weight in gold) was an engraving of St Paul's Cathedral from the south side of the Thames. The engraving belonged to Sir Ernest Shackleton and had been carried by him on every one of his expeditions – it was even in his cabin on *Endurance*, in the *James Caird* and in his cabin when he died. It was given to me by a member of the Shackleton family as a talisman (in turn, I presented it to the officers and crew of HMS *Endurance* when we reached Spitsbergen). Our talisman now hangs in its original frame in the wardroom and has served the ship well.

In time, of course, we grew accustomed to the sounds and the vibrations of grinding ice floes, and it was seldom that our daily walks did not reveal a new fracture in the floe. But on 1 November, just as we were settling down again to a peaceful state of mind, the track of our drift changed direction.

'This painting shows two of us checking the floe for new cracks in the dead of winter on the Arctic Ocean. No polar explorers, before us or since, have ever spent several months at that latitude drifting through the polar night, constantly in danger.

'At 85 degrees north in the winter it is dark most of the time, except for when you have moonlight or an aurora, and this is the main light source in this painting. The hut is the focal point of the picture, with Allan Gill and me walking towards the hut with the aurora cloud sweeping around and appearing to be pointing a finger. We are also carrying Tilley lamps, creating the yellow pools of light.

'This painting is absolutely unique, for by the position of the stars above the horizon it is possible to see the latitude of the winter camp – the focal point of the painting.'

Throughout the rest of the winter, while the floes cracked up around us and while we worked 15 hours a day on the scientific programme and our preparations for the final dash to Spitsbergen, we drifted eastwards. By 3 February l969, our hut was again dangerously situated, this time in a wedge of two fractures that were only 140 yards from the hut. On the morning of 24 February, two hours before we were due to have started loading the sledges, the floe cracked up like an eggshell and the whole area started to gyrate. The nearest fracture had split the floe only 3 yards from the hut. We abandoned it and in semi-darkness scrambled around rescuing our dogs and sledges as the ice pans heaved under our feet.

The North Pole and Beyond

Navigating by the moon and Venus we headed north. We were almost 400 miles behind schedule and the temperature was around -45 degrees Centigrade. Sledges, dogs and men were faced with their toughest test. Finally, on 6 April l969 (by coincidence the 60th anniversary of the date Cdr Robert E. Peary claimed, falsely, that he had reached that same desolate spot), we reached the North Pole. Actually, by dead reckoning, I had calculated that we had reached the Pole the day before, and had sent a radio message to Her Majesty The Queen (by Morse Code via Squadron Leader Freddy Church in Point Barrow) that I had the pleasure to inform Her Majesty that we had reached the North Pole.

However, no sooner had I sent the message than the sun came out (for the first time in several days) and I was able to get a fix on our position – and would you believe it: we were not at the North Pole, but still 7 miles from it! And so we had broken camp and travelled in a great hurry the extra 7 miles in the hope of getting to the Pole before the date changed. But in our hurry, we had gone slightly in the wrong direction, and so by the time we had got ourselves back on track, the date had changed to the 6th, and I now had a 'link' with Peary – the first of many, as I was later to discover.

Shortly after reaching the Pole we had our final air-drop of supplies. Heading south (for the first time in over 13 months) I now had the feeling that I was, in a sense, descending from the summit – heading towards a darkening horizon. Whether this was a premonition, or simply the strain of the journey, I do not know. One thing, however, was certain: it was only by forced marches that we could now reach Spitsbergen before the summer melt began; and then came the mists, the broken floes, the ordeal of 15-hour marches, the anxieties, and the fatigue.

Seldom in the history of polar exploration has such a sense of urgency possessed men and dogs; seldom was there a goal more attractive than the solid land 600 miles to our south. It had become a race we could win only by driving ourselves and our dogs to the very limit of physical endurance – and against all odds, our efforts were rewarded.

We sighted land at the end of our 16-month journey (by coincidence) at precisely the moment that the astronaut Jack Young (of *Apollo 12*) took that now-famous photo of the *Earthrise* from the moon; and at 19.00 hrs GMT on 29 May (on the 13th anniversary of Hillary and Tensing reaching the summit

of Mount Everest) a landing was made by Allan Gill and Major Ken Hedges RAMC on a small rocky island at latitude 80.49 N, longitude 20.23 E, after a scramble across three-quarters of a mile of mush ice and gyrating ice pans.

That landing, though brief, concluded the first surface crossing of the Arctic Ocean – a journey of 3,620 route miles from Point Barrow, Alaska, via the Pole of Inaccessibility and the North Pole. That landing also completed the 'trilogy' of the last three great geographical 'firsts' in the history of human endeavour: namely, the first ascent of the highest mountain in the world, and the first surface crossing of the southern and northern icecaps of the Earth.

We were committed to travel for a further ten days (and more than 100 route miles) before we were able to reach HMS *Endurance*, and could be lifted aboard. From land to land that journey had taken 464 days, and yet, oddly enough, its climax was not the sight of land, but the sight from land of the ice across which we had come.

'There were only a few hours of twilight at that time of the year and it was extremely dangerous ice that we would be travelling on during the next few weeks.'

Setting Out from Point Barrow (watercolour)

'This is based on the only photograph that was taken of setting out from Point Barrow, Alaska, with all four teams of dogs in the picture. The photographer was Frank Hermann of The Sunday Times. *With this painting I tried to capture the feeling of being under a 'spotlight' of public attention – there were only a few hours of twilight at that time of the year and it was extremely dangerous ice that we would be travelling on during the next few weeks.'*

Polar Bear on Misty Pack Ice (watercolour)

'This painting was based on an idea that worried me quite a bit on the Arctic Ocean. In the wintertime we had to patrol the ice floes to see whether the ice was cracking up around us and there was always a possibility of a bear being behind the next pressure ridge. Our chances of seeing one were slim, because it is only lonely male bears that wander around the Arctic Ocean, but nevertheless it was a possibility and so this painting was to represent those few times where you go for a walk, climb up a pressure ridge and find yourself confronted by a bear.'

Polar Bear Lying on New Ice (oils)

'The person who commissioned this painting asked me to paint a bear lying down, but he was adamant that the bear should not look as though it were dead! I decided to make the bear look playful, full of life, and painted him on freshly formed ice; the fathoms of water underneath the new ice gives it an unusual darkness and depth.'

North Pole Group No. 2, 6 April 1969 (oils)

Based on the 2nd photograph taken on 6 April 1969, showing the group at the North Pole. Left to right: Dr Fritz Koerner, Major Ken Hedges RAMC, Allan Gill and Wally Herbert.

Portrait of Cdr Robert E. Peary (pencil & scalpel)

'The portrait of Peary on the left is a magical one. It was done in 1987 as the dust-jacket for my synopsis of the book The Noose of Laurels, inspired by a famous portrait of Peary where he is dressed up in his furs. The drawing was done in about six hours, non-stop. It was quite amazing just how fast that one came about.

'The thing with those portraits is that as I study the portrait from which I am doing the picture, I find I get under the skin of the person. You see their personality, much more so I think than if you do a portrait of them when they are just posing, and this is why I usually prefer using photographs to using a live sitter; possibly also because of my memory of the first woman that I drew a portrait of who passed out and bumped her head and was unconscious for several minutes on the floor. So from then on I have never ever drawn live portraits for fear that they might pass out.

'The advantage of doing a portrait from a photograph is that you can choose a photograph that suits you – if necessary you can even create a three-dimensional photograph of the sitter so you can see their ears and look at them from different angles. You can also get images of the sitter smiling or with another expression on their face, instead of looking bored and tired. There are very few sitters who can stay still enough to get that photographic effect. With a camera you can capture those intimate little moments.

'In my portrait of Peary, his eyes seem to reveal a man under intense stress – much more so through my portrait than through the photograph. My portrait seems to reveal a secret – as though there is something distressing him.

'When the portrait was finished I had it photographed and framed and put on the wall. Eventually I took it with me on one of my trips up to the Arctic on an icebreaker – the ship was going to travel from Mermansk to the North Pole then across the Arctic Ocean to the Bering Strait. So, the day before we got to the North Pole, I announced to the passengers that the following day, at the North Pole, I was going to put the portrait down into the sea through a hole in the ice unless it was sold, and thankfully someone bought it!'

North Pole Group No. 1, 6 April 1969 (watercolour)

Right, based on the official photograph taken on 6 April 1969 at the North Pole by Wally Herbert (using the self-timing device on the camera). Left to right: Wally Herbert, Dr Fritz Koerner, Allan Gill and Major Ken Hedges RAMC.

North Pole — 6th April 1969

Crossing the North Pole
(oils)

'This painting was composed out of three pictures clipped from a 35mm film of the day we arrived at the North Pole. If you look closely you can see that it is the same team three times, but with one sledge only; the dogs constantly weave between each other, so although the dogs are the same, they are in different places within the team. I am at the back of the sledge, then following in the distance are the other three sledges.

'The significance of this painting is that it is a representation of the moment of crossing the North Pole, not arriving at the North Pole. Interestingly enough the sun is at 6% above the horizon, which is accurate from the many observations we did at the North Pole. The ice too is the ice we actually saw at the North Pole.

'So the sun in this position is blinding, with rays of light coming down, as if you are looking at the painting through a lens. It looks as though we are going through a shower of light – with rays of light radiating down – I made this more obvious by making some of the dogs "disappear" as they are bleached out by the light as they cross the Pole. The sun is in fact representing the North Pole, because of its exact angle above the horizon. Then, by virtue of the fact that these rays of light are coming down at an angle from the sun, they are representative of the lines of longitude, which is exactly what you get when you are reaching the North Pole.

'This seemed to me a much more natural way of seeing the moment of crossing the Pole.'

Landfall on Svalbard 1969
(oils)

'This painting is a composite picture of the actual scene of heading towards land after 16 months on the ice. My dog team in the foreground is following the tracks of the three dog teams that have gone ahead; they are in among the pack ice so you can't see them.

'Not long before this moment, I was at the back of the column of four sledges, which was my usual position as leader (to ensure that none of my companions ran into trouble), and I was just curious if there was any sighting of land. We were navigators so we were able to tell where we were, and we knew when we should see land, plus or minus a day (depending on cloud, refraction and mirages of course), but we knew roughly when we would see land and that is the reason why we were looking on that particular day.

'So, I climbed a pressure ridge and stuck a harpoon into the ice, levelled the telescope of the rifle against this harpoon, looked through the telescopic sight, and there was this magical scene. That moment inspired this painting, although the painting shows us being a good deal closer to land. But it nevertheless represents the moment of truth for the expedition — the moment when we made landfall, and fulfilled the purpose of the expedition.'

'I climbed a pressure ridge and stuck a harpoon into the ice, levelled the telescope of the rifle against this harpoon, looked through the telescopic sight, and there was this magical scene.'

Jumping Bear – a Polar Bear Jumping a Fracture in the Ice (oils)

'We were visited by several polar bears during the summer – all of them were hungry, and none of them could easily be driven off.'

Reaching Land (Herbert Island) 29 May 1969 (watercolour)

'The story of the actual moment of the landing is told through the painting on the right of the mother bear and her two cubs standing on a pressure ridge, looking at the island on which we landed. The tracks of the bears, intersecting with the tracks of the sledge, lead you into the painting, then the eye-line of the bears draws the eye to the distance where you can see our sledges approaching land.

'The bears, of course, are natural to that environment, and they are watching these four men – intruders in that setting – walking towards land. Here we have four "aliens" in total ignorance of the presence of the bears. For the men this is the high point of their career; they are going to make a landing on this island and complete the first surface crossing of the Arctic Ocean, and yet the bears have been walking over the Arctic Ocean for centuries, and the young cubs will be doing just that for the rest of their lives. So, it makes a nice statement of how insignificant we are in comparison to these kings of the Arctic.'

TILTING AT ICEBERGS

*'On finding that the only solution to surviving in the frozen north was to regard the dark period
as his dominant season and the sea with its treacherous skin of ice as his "natural" element, the
Polar Eskimo not only managed to adapt to this harsh setting, but in the process produced the most
distinctive and brilliant hunting culture that the world has ever known.'*

WALLY HERBERT, *ESKIMOS*, 1976

WE ARRIVED BACK AT PORTSMOUTH (the home port of HMS *Endurance*) to a muted reception; for as the last of the old-style pioneering journeys made by men on the face of the Earth ended, the eyes of the world were focused on an event of far greater historical significance – the first landing on the moon. There was nothing to do except throw myself into the task of completing the film *Across the Top of the World* for the BBC and recording the official account of the expedition.

A few more months went by before that subtle reminder of my marital status finally got through to me and Marie, whom I had met when planning the expedition, accepted my proposal of marriage (in the car park at Terminal Three of London's Heathrow Airport). We were married three days later, on Christmas Eve 1969, at Chelsea Registry Office – Marie looking stunning in a thigh-length Alaskan fur parka, a mini-skirt and long white boots. Needless to say, there was no time for a honeymoon as I had a deadline to finish a book; instead, a year-and-a-half later, I took Marie and our new addition to the family – my daughter Kari – up to Northwest Greenland and introduced them to the Polar World.

Hunter & the Narwhal (oils) [pages 124–25]

My idea was to record on film, and in a book, the 'dying culture' of the Polar Eskimos – an idea inspired by Robert Flaherty' *Nanook of the North*. We were to live among these, the northernmost people in the world, as inconspicuously as possible, fitting in with their way of life, eating whatever they ate, dressing in whatever they dressed in, and speaking their native language. Of course, it was a naive idea; but we went to it with a will, and in time we were accepted by that little hunting community of 16 adults and as many children as a 'natural' part of the scene – indeed we have even become a part of the folklore of the Polar Eskimos. This, I am bound to say, was mainly due to Marie and Kari who, to my surprise and relief, settled in almost immediately to living in the squalid conditions of an Eskimo hunter's hut and having our privacy invaded at any time of the day or night by roguish Eskimo children. But then, this was perhaps the main reason why we settled in so quickly – we learnt the language through the children, and through them got to know their parents.

Unlike for my new family, Northwest Greenland was a place that was quite familiar to me; I had already spent many months in the area – either buying dogs

Hunter & the Polar Bear
(oils)

*'This is a painting depicting
the ancient tradition of
hunting bear by lance. It is
an extraordinary sight to see
– the strength and power of
the bear pitted against the
skill of the hunter. Hunting
by lance is by far the most
dangerous way to hunt bears,
with only a few hunters
skilled enough to attempt it.'*

from the Eskimo hunters for expeditions in the Antarctic, or training for the Trans-Arctic Expedition.

Among the persisting memories of my first visit to Northwest Greenland in 1966, one in particular always affected me deeply. I had merely taken one step beyond the northern limits of the village of Siorapaluk – the most northerly village in the world – then turned to gaze idly over the frozen waters of the fjord on which it lies. It did not occur to me for some moments that there was anything significant in what I had done. But then, suddenly, I realized that in taking that single step I had placed myself north of every native man, woman and child on the face of the Earth. I have seldom experienced such a glorious feeling of pride.

Since then I have travelled much farther north, to the Pole itself, and the delight I experienced in Siorapaluk now strikes me as somewhat naive. Yet hidden within the pride I felt that day lies the essential clue to the survival of the Polar Eskimos. The unique position this extraordinary people occupy as the northernmost community on Earth gives them a sense of being superior to other men. In triumphing over the hardships of their Arctic environment – the bitter cold, the frequent exposure to danger and the threat of hunger – the Polar Eskimos believe that they have demonstrated their pre-eminence over dwellers in more temperate lands, who do not have to face such challenges. Without that conviction, I believe, they would long ago have

found themselves on the same downward spiral that all other Eskimo groups began early in the last century.

The region that the Polar Eskimos inhabit is known to Westerners as Thule, a name bestowed on it by the Danish explorer Knud Rasmussen, after the legendary land that the ancient Greeks believed lay at the northernmost limits of the habitable world. The Thule District lies between 75° and 80° latitude on the rugged northwest coast of Greenland. Constitutionally part of Denmark, Greenland is the largest island on Earth, with a deeply indented 24,500-mile coastline – almost equal in total length to the equatorial circumference of the planet. Yet it is also one of the most sparsely populated areas of the world: more than 80 per cent of the island is covered by a lifeless ice sheet that is over a mile thick for most of its extent. The total population of the country is only about 55,000, of whom some 750 are Polar Eskimos.

Even by the standards of this vast and desolate island, the Thule region is remote. It is a small oasis of habitable land in a surrounding desert of ice. To visit their nearest neighbours in the south, the Polar Eskimos must make a journey of 400 miles along the uninhabited coastline of Melville Bay. Their territory is bounded to the west by the headwaters of Baffin Bay. Northwards, there is no sign of life between them and the Pole, more than 800 miles away, except for a few archaeological sites along Greenland's north coast – evidence that once, long ago, the territory was less hostile to man than it is today. To

Shaman & His Dogs
(watercolour)

'Taitianguaraitsiak was the old man who lived next to us on Herbert Island. He was the father of Avatak, and interestingly enough Avatak had been born on the same day as myself, so we used to joke that if circumstances had been different I could have been his son. I don't know quite how that works out, but he was a father-figure to me in many ways.'

the east, the uninhabitable Greenland ice sheet stretches 600 miles or more. In theory, it is possible for the Polar Eskimos to meet with their fellow-countrymen on the east coast by skirting the ice sheet's northern edge; but to do so they would have to embark on a hazardous 2,500-mile journey that I myself attempted with my companion Allan Gill in 1978 and which I can testify passes through barren wastelands for most of the way.

My burgeoning interest in arctic exploration had originally brought me to the district. At the time of my first visit to Siorapaluk, I was outward-bound with two companions on our 1,500-mile journey to retrace the route of the pioneer explorer Dr Frederick Cook, a route we had chosen as training for our British Trans-Arctic Expedition, which was to be mounted the following year.

I still recall with amusement and embarrassment the affectionate concern shown to us by the Eskimos with whom we wintered. None of them believed we would succeed, and several even marked crosses on our maps to indicate the exact position where they predicted we would perish. We did successfully complete the journey and duly returned to Thule the following winter, where we enjoyed the pleasures of a friendly reunion with our surprised Eskimo friends. Since then I have returned to the region many times and, in the course

of these visits, the Thule district has become almost a second home to me. The more I learn about these hardy people, the greater is the respect I hold for them.

Temperamentally the Polar Eskimos are well-attuned to the world in which they live. They are natural stoics, who instinctively impose a tight discipline upon their actions and emotions. Though they react quickly when circumstances demand it, their self-control in moments of real danger – on breaking sea-ice, say, in the middle of a storm – is wonderful to behold.

The obverse of this tight mental discipline is the raucous humour that is one of their most endearing characteristics. An irrepressible sense of fun will burst out at the most solemn moments, expressing itself in practical jokes and slapstick of every kind. As an Eskimo bends over, intent on some minor chore, a friend will creep up behind him and seize him by the calf, revelling in his victim's momentary panic as he thinks a rogue dog has him in its jaws.

Polar Night

The territory that the Polar Eskimos inhabit confounds all the expectations of uninformed visitors from the south. To begin with, the characteristics of its season differ more radically than anything experienced in temperate lands.

Each winter, from late October to February, the Polar Eskimos experience four months of permanent darkness while the Earth is tilted away from the sun. Correspondingly, in summer, from mid-April to August, they are compensated with four months of continuous daylight when the sun is north of the equator. Only in the intermediate periods – the spring and autumn – do the Polar Eskimos enjoy the alternation of light and darkness within a 24-hour span that most of the world takes for granted.

It is impossible for any non-Eskimo, accustomed to the diurnal balance of night and day, to appreciate the sensation of the four-month polar night; the fear of continuous darkness felt by men of temperate latitudes is primeval in its origins and almost inconsolable. Yet, to the Eskimos and those few explorers who have spent several years in the Polar regions within 15° latitude of the North or South Poles, the long night is a magical period. Although there is no sunlight, the darkness is far from total. The light of the moon and the stars is not only reflected but magnified by the enveloping snow and ice, contradicting the very concept of darkness and lightening the heart.

The long polar night is a bewitching time of year to journey by sledge – a time that burns its brand on a traveller and makes him forever a man of the Arctic. The experience of moving across a seeming infinity of sea-ice in the winter darkness has an almost mystical quality. There is no setting in the world more beautiful than a polar ice-scape illuminated by a full moon high in a cloudless sky, and no Polar Eskimo child every forgets his first awareness of this weird and unearthly light.

There is an unforgettable excitement in travelling in pitch-darkness without stars or a compass to serve as a guide. At this time of year, I have journeyed with the Polar Eskimos in the most fearful conditions imaginable. At first I was amazed by their ability to pick a tortuous route through the night. I marvelled, for example, at a hunter who could make his way in the darkness up a frozen glacial cataract to a height of 2,500 feet, cross a high pass

Three Faces of an Eskimo Shaman (pencil & scalpel)

'A drawing of our neighbour on Herbert Island in Northwest Greenland in 1971–73. Taitianguaraitsiak was the first of the Herbert Islanders ever to invite us out to do anything that was natural, that was part of their tradition, when he went to lay nets under the new sea ice.

'He was a wonderful old man and he became a very dear friend of the family. My daughter Kari called him "Aata", meaning grandfather.

'This portrait was an attempt to capture the emotion of parting in the dead of winter as it appeared on the face of this dear old soul as he turned away from the light of civilization to return to his home, and we to ours. When the other hunters in the village saw the picture they believed it proved that he was a shaman, and that the picture showed him turning towards the spirit world.'

Three Polar Bears Passing the Camp of Sleeping Hunters (watercolour)

'This painting was based on an experience I had in Smith Sound between Greenland and Ellesmere Island when I was travelling with some hunters. They persuaded me that night to go into the tent with them to sleep on their sleeping platform. I asked them about bears and they said, "bears never come anywhere near the dogs". The next morning when we got up we found bear tracks – a bear and two cubs had actually walked past the dogs, within a few yards of the dogs, while they were sleeping.

'In this painting the rising sun is lighting up the scene in a pink glow with three bears walking silently past these dogs and the tent with the hunters sleeping.'

in swirling mist and then, almost intuitively, set a course to take him through a field of crevasses to the one solitary point where the terrain allowed him to cross a moraine and enter a gully that, by way of innumerable twists and turns, led steeply down to a frozen fjord a thousand feet below.

Eventually, by harsh experience, I came to understand how this was possible. In the blackest night, the skilled hunter derives useful information from the many seemingly trivial things: the way the snow lies, the direction of the wind, the angle at which his sledge is tilting. Every detail of the landscape is registered on his memory. His secret is having intimate knowledge of his Polar World, respecting its warning signs and knowing his own limitations.

It is during the first few weeks of the long polar night that one sees most strikingly how the basic pattern of life in Thule has remained unchanged for centuries. In their pursuit of seal and walrus over the thin sea-ice, the hunters employ methods developed by their most distant ancestors. In turn, their brief hunt provides a mountain of work for their wives, who use age-old techniques to scrape and clean sealskins, then cut up the hides to make outer clothing for travelling.

Every hunter looks forward to realizing the dream that all polar hunters have cherished over the ages: the urge to harness up their dogs and enjoy the

exhilarating sense of freedom that comes with sledging on their own far out across the ice in quest of seal or walrus.

My first experience of hunting walrus in the long polar night is still a vivid memory. Towards the end of January, I had set off from Herbert Island in the company of my friend Avatak, the hunter. We were journeying over the ice of Whale Sound, heading for the coast of Steensby Land, where we hoped to find walrus at their breathing-holes in the new ice. As we moved off, I looked up at the sky and saw, at long last, a pale refracted hint of the returning sun.

In the bitter cold, with the fog of breath streaming from the dogs, we travelled for some four hours until, in the far distance, I saw two sledges – one of them covered with a makeshift tent held up by two harpoons stuck in the snow. When we drew alongside this sledge, we found that the occupants of the tent were Avatak's septuagenarian father, Taitianguaraitsiak, and his wife, who were snuggled inside, drinking mugs of tea brewed on a primus stove. My hunting companion, who was busy untangling the traces of his dogs, told me to go and join them. For half an hour I shared the fug of steam and warmth within the tent. Then, shortly before we moved on, I asked the old man where he was heading. He did not say. He simply chuckled and replied, 'Maybe we, too, will hunt the walrus.'

His wife sighed. 'But the walrus will hear you breathing and go away.'
'Then, woman,' he growled, 'I shall hold my breath.'

He immediately proceeded to give us a demonstration, holding his breath until he was blue in the face and had scared us half to death. Finally, after what seemed an eternity, he gasped out air and burst into raucous laughter.

The next day, having invited the old folk to join us, we did get our walrus. Avatak led the way, while we ventured cautiously in his footsteps over the new ice that stretched for about a mile from the coast. Eventually we came to an area scarred with many holes, each 2 or 3 feet across. I wondered how such large holes had been created, and I was about to ask when my question was answered: less than 20 feet away the enormous head and tusks of a bull walrus – representing one and a half tons of meat and blubber – smashed through the thin ice. It gazed short-sightedly in our direction for several seconds with its startled, bloodshot eyes, then sank out of sight.

I have never felt more vulnerable. Twice more the walrus surfaced, each time a little nearer to us. My companions signalled me not to move; and for three minutes – the longest three minutes of my life – I remained rooted to the spot. Then, at last, the walrus surfaced a fourth time, only 10 feet away. Avatak was ready. He rushed forward and thrust his harpoon deep into the walrus's neck. As the beast sank back into the sea, Avatak took up his ice pick, drove it into the soft new ice, looped the harpoon line round it, then braced his foot against the handle of the pick as the line played out.

Eskimo Hunter and Walrus (oils)

'This was taken from my experience of seeing Avatak standing on very thin ice, and reaching over to pull a walrus out of the sea.'

By far the most difficult part of the hunt was hauling the dead walrus onto the sea-ice. We used two teams of dogs and a block and tackle, but when the 12 foot-long walrus was almost halfway out of the water, the surrounding ice began to give way under its enormous weight. Avatak at once climbed on to the back of the walrus and opened up the carcass along its length with his knife so that, on our next attempt, its weight would be more widely distributed on the ice. His cunning did the trick; the dogs strained against the end of their traces, and all at once the carcass came free.

In the fading light, Avatak gathered a ball of snow and placed it in the mouth of the carcass, honouring the spirit of the animal, and ensuring that the spirit would not go thirsty on its way to the next realm.

A few weeks later, in mid-February, I was still travelling with Avatak when the polar night ended. Our sledges had temporarily become separated and when I caught up with him, I witnessed something I have never seen again in all my subsequent visits to the Arctic. In the far distance, I saw him performing his own private greeting to the returning sun.

For a few minutes, Avatak stood gazing at the sun as it slowly crept above the horizon. As its light flooded across the silvery plain, he pushed back the hood of his parka and bared his head. Throwing his hands high, he turned the palms outwards so that they were bathed in the brilliant red glow, before finally placing them on his head. Avatak did not know I was watching him. For a long time I did not move for fear of revealing my presence and so marring what was clearly a personal and spiritual moment. In that moving gesture, when he celebrated the end of the four long months of darkness, it was as though he and the sun were one in spirit – and its warmth and light gave him fresh hope and energy, just as surely as it infused new life into the Polar World.

Seeking Fulfilment

Even though those two years living, travelling and hunting with the Polar Eskimos had been magical on many levels it was not, however, the sort of experience I believed I had at that time been needing; for although I sledged well over 4,000 miles and over every known route within 300 miles of Herbert Island (always with my own team of dogs), and had learnt a great deal from my native companions, my journeys had all been through territory they knew like the backs of their hands – thus denying me in some strange way any personal sense of achievement. These confusions, combined with the fact that my father died while we were up in Northwest Greenland, deeply affected me – although I would not admit it at the time. I was to learn later that he had burnt all the newspaper clippings which celebrated his sporting achievements as a young man because he felt I would not have wanted them since I had so many clippings of my own achievements in the North. If only I had told him how much I really admired him – but I had thought there would be time.

These struggles were intensified by what I can only describe as a 'love-hate' relationship with the Eskimo hunters, with whom I had risked my life on

many occasions. The irony was never more poignant than when my Eskimo travelling companions would treat me as one of their own, for example, by leaving me to fend for myself in the pitch blackness of midwinter on a walrus hunt, or on a plateau in a blizzard. I could never accept that this was a sign of their utmost respect, because my own way of doing things was so very different.

Marie, of course, could see it all: 'In the company of Eskimos, Wally was frustrated by his lack of "native skill", and frustrated by the subordinate role – to follow and observe. It became for him a discipline to watch the techniques of the hunters through the lenses of his cameras, and he had learnt a lot about them he might otherwise have missed. But with filming he felt unfulfilled, and he was never completely at ease with his Eskimo companions. Some said they understood him, for although his feelings had few words, they read him through his signs. But they could not know the optimist, the raconteur, the man whose bawdy sense of humour and the pathos of his tales can, as if by magic, change the colour of the world. They could not know his "need" to make another long and hazardous polar journey, or the reason why that journey must be longer and more difficult than the last; but they wanted to go with him to make certain he succeeded, and a more ironic compliment was never paid a man.'

And so, eventually, we came home – back to the world we thought we knew, and which our daughter Kari had never ever known. Her first language had been a dialect of Eskimo – spoken only by the Thule people. True enough, she could understand what Marie and I were saying to her in English, but she would always reply in Eskimo because that, to her, was more natural since it was the language of her Eskimo playmates, and of course, she missed them sorely

Four years went by before I returned once again to the Polar World, for a serious back injury had banged the door shut on my plans for a circum-navigation of the world – or rather, a 'completion' of that journey by starting from the point where the journey across the top of the world had ended – namely, from Spitsbergen back to Alaska via the South Pole. That back injury also put an end to another plan I had been working on for some time: a solo circumpolar journey from North Cape in Norway right through Siberia, across the frozen Bering Strait, and the Canadian Arctic to the Northeastern tip of Greenland. Bold plans indeed, and at the root of them, no doubt, was the desire to make a really 'special' journey. But such dreams were clearly a waste of time. Far more sensibly, I eventually realized, this 'energy' should be directed into writing a book. And so, I started a book entitled *Polar Eskimos*, a book that was to win the German State Literary Prize for 1977, and it was this book that led me towards the 'swan song' of my polar career.

The First Circumnavigation of Greenland 1977–79

No other journey comes anywhere near to being as hazardous or as quixotic as that 1977–79 attempt by dog sledge and Eskimo skin boat to make the first circumnavigation of Greenland with my old partner, Allan Gill. With Allan now pushing 46 and myself only four years younger, this clearly was to be our last expedition. We also had good reason for believing that this would be physically the hardest journey we had ever undertaken, for even the 3,800-mile trek we had made in 1968–69 from Alaska to Spitsbergen via the North Pole had only been half the distance of the one that we were now contemplating.

As with all such journeys, there was a long and exhausting period of planning and fund-raising – and in this case also a trip to Alaska to buy a whaling boat (an Eskimo *umiak*) from the hunters at Point Barrow. It had then to be dismantled, crated and flown back to Britain for onward shipment via Copenhagen to Mestersvig on the east coast of Greenland. Depots of food and fuel needed to be laid all around the Greenland coastline almost two full years in advance, and the money in those days was hard to come by – particularly so in the case of this project because no one seemed to be in the slightest bit interested.

And yet, here was a venture that not only offered the perfect setting for an epic polar expedition, but was also one of the most interesting journeys that a polar traveller could make – a journey for which by way of preparation Allan and I had sledged a total of over 23,000 miles across some of the toughest routes in both the Arctic and the Antarctic. It was, in fact, a challenge

Dogs Scent a Bear (watercolour)

'In every team of dogs belonging to Eskimo hunters there are the "bear dogs" – those that have been trained by the hunters, when released or cut free from their traces, to go after the bear and stop it from escaping into the sea. These bear dogs are never sold to a white man.'

towards which every polar journey we had made in the past 20 years had inevitably been leading.

It was an expedition that had already been fully five years in the planning and the countdown had begun by the time we had discovered that Marie was a few weeks pregnant, and so there was no possibility of cancelling the project. But although Marie had insisted that she would not stand in the way if I really felt I had to go, I was torn apart by those two obligations, and had set off for Greenland cursing the very grail I was seeking.

Allan and I set out for Northwest Greenland early in the winter of 1977, followed shortly after by Mai Zetterling (the famous Hollywood film star and director), whose intention it was to make a film documentary, appropriately, on the theme of 'Obsession'. She had a belief that her energy came directly as a result of a lightning strike, and this energy she recharged from time to time by deliberately attracting these strikes. Sadly, the BBC was faced with an industrial dispute at that time over the number of people that should be employed in a film crew, so this seriously affected Mai's plans and the film was never made. But she was a fascinating and very original lady and I benefited greatly from her wisdom and optimism.

On 27 January 1970, with two very large teams of dogs, we finally set out from Dundas, near Thule Airbase, and for the next 200 miles we were in territory we had passed through many times over the years. But up near the entrance to the Robeson Channel we ran into the first of our many problems. Here the sea-ice was very thin, badly fractured and extremely dangerous, and it was here, in this lethal-looking spot, that our camp was hit by a hurricane-force wind. It was screeching across the 6 inches of ice on which our tent was precariously pitched and blowing straight out to the open sea. With the ice bending visibly under our weight, we expected to survive no more than ten minutes. But that blizzard raged for 36 hours and by the time it had blown itself out, Allan and I were near total wrecks. For that 36 hours we had not

Three Huskies, Northwest Greenland (watercolour)

'These three dogs belonged to Taitianguaraitsiak, the old shaman and our next door neighbour. They were far too strong for him to handle in his last few years, but he was reluctant to let them go as they were his pride and joy.'

been able to speak to each other because of the noise of the flapping tent, which had also given us splitting headaches and had made it impossible to light the stove, or to have anything to eat or drink. We had no choice but to sit there shivering – convinced by the reflected fear that we could see in each other's eyes that we had only minutes to live. Small wonder then that when the wind finally eased enough for us to be able to shout above it, the first spoken words were: 'never again', 'never, ever again!'.

We eventually reached Alert (a Distant Early Warning Station at the northeastern tip of Ellesmere Island) and there, on 30 March 1978, I received the news that Marie had given birth to Pascale. The news for me was an emotional watershed, for ever since leaving home seven months earlier, I had been racked with guilt, and I sensed from the occasional letters received from Marie and Kari, that they were lonely and confused. I too felt that what I was doing was inexcusably 'wrong', and yet overriding that feeling was a powerful compulsion – an 'obsession' I guess – and a certain sense of 'mission' that had me totally in its grip.

I was fast approaching the lowest ebb in my life, for in spite of the relief and pride that I felt at the news of Pascale's birth, my 'dream', at that time, seemed on the very brink of collapsing.

A few days out from Alert I struck rock bottom – it was a depression that, fortunately I guess, coincided with a six-day storm which held us trapped in a hunter's hut, and so in a sense there was no time wasted. But it was an alarming experience that had shaken hard at my belief system, and at what I was striving in vain to achieve.

Our journey from there on descended into one of the most colourful episodes of misery that either Allan or I had ever encountered, and by the time we had travelled some 1,600 miles and had reached a peninsula called Hold With Hope, we were running out of time, and food.

'Hold With Hope' was the name that Henry Hudson had given to this rugged peninsula in 1607 – a name to encourage the confidence of his crew perhaps. Little did he know how many men over the years, both seafarers and dog sledgers, would smile wryly at the unintentional mockery in this name, for there comes a time, as history had shown and our own experience now began to confirm, when hope is a dangerous diversion from the realities of life and the only chance of surviving is to grit one's teeth and curse.

And so we cursed that stretch of coast – and not without good reason, for there was not a clean place on that north coast to camp. The sea-ice was cracked up and covered in mud, and the beach that looked firm a footstep away turned out to be a strip of ooze into which we sank up to our shins and from which it took us several hours to extricate ourselves. By then it was midsummer's day. The black rain clouds were thickening and rolling across the rotten ice; every item of equipment and clothing, every dog and every exposed square inch of human flesh was covered in wet mud and blue-grey slime. But although we made 5 miles that day, having got back onto the sea-ice once again in a desperate effort to reach Loch Fyne, we then spent three nerve-racking days in trying to get off it. The ice had suddenly started to break up and peel away from the coast, the rain had been falling in torrents and the melt streams were roaring down from the hills and rattling boulders along their beds that would have smashed any sledge, or dog, or human leg that happened to get in the way.

Boat Passing Iceberg (watercolour)

We had, therefore, no sooner escaped from one problem than we had found ourselves facing another. Our sledges, in those conditions, were far too heavy; we could not budge them an inch without offloading half of the gear and hitching all 25 dogs to one sledge, and after about 4 miles of this and several days of murderous toil, during which we covered those same 4 miles a total of no fewer than seven times, it had become pretty obvious to us that we were in need of a new technique. And so we built two small sledges out of skis and bits of driftwood; but these had proved to be too weak and had not survived the first river delta we had to cross. We then spent a few days making pack frames out of bone, string, driftwood and ski sticks so that we could take some of the weight of our load on our backs and reduce the strain on our makeshift sledges – and this combination, though slow and crippling, we finally adopted as the only way that we could make any progress across the steaming tundra. Even then, every mile had to be covered three times by each of us, and the journey became a struggle as unique and dramatic as it was gruelling.

By 10 July we had rounded the southern end of Loch Fyne across the baked mudflats of Badlandal. We had been eaten alive by the swarms of mosquitoes and half-drowned in the thundering rivers. We had been blasted raw by choking sandstorms that even in Tolkien's 'Middle Earth' would hardly have seemed more sinister, for what we had come through had been, in truth, a real and damn-nearly lethal nightmare in which we were tormented and reduced by fatigue to the very brink of insanity. In our fight to defend our breathing space there had been times when we thought the end had come and the mosquitoes in their blood-filled millions finally had won; but in our spluttering and near-hysterical defiance we had cursed and raged and staggered on, flailing the air with arms and whips and hacking a pathway through those mosquitoes, until the wind-blown sand had swept down the valley and blown them all to Hell.

We had covered our faces and pushed through those sandstorms, and hauled our sledges across the baked mud-flats under a canopy of hanging dust through which the sun shone weakly yellow and stained the world in a colour so unreal it was almost as though we were hauling our sledges on the face of a different planet. But by then we were so tired and hungry, and so sick with smoking dried tea leaves, that this seemed like the end of the road.

And so the story goes on and on – the 'swan song' of two ageing polar explorers, the one a 'visionary', the other a 'pragmatist' – two men 'tilting at windmills'. This 'adventure' was quite unlike any other I have ever lived through.

On reaching Mestersvig (halfway down the east coast of Greenland) Marie, Kari and baby Pascale were there, much to our surprise, to greet us – and the reunion with my now larger family (from which I had been separated for every day of the past eleven months) was absolutely wonderful. There we were to spend about a month together while Allan and I were preparing for the boating stage of our journey and waiting for the ice to break out of the sound, and never once did Marie openly question my decision to continue that crazy journey. But that question was asked of me every day through their love and support, and their silence on this issue. They 'knew' that I had a binding commitment to complete the journey, and the saddest day in my life (up till then) was the day that Allan and I set out from Mestersvig in the umiak with Marie, Kari and baby Pascale left behind on the quay.

The adventures and the heart-searchings of those next few weeks wound up this 'chapter' of my life – this final challenge in a physical sense, before the dawn of wisdom. Subconsciously, perhaps for the past 14 years, I had been listening, watching, and speaking with nature. I had also subconsciously been learning from travelling with Peter and Avatak – two of the finest long-range hunters of

Allan Gill's Dog Team on the Arctic Ocean
(watercolour)

'Allan's dog team on the Arctic Ocean as the weather begins to warm up with the approach of summer.'

the world's most northerly Eskimo tribe – both of whom had lost their lives in tragic circumstances. I had last seen Avatak on the day we left Qaanaaq heading north, and had last seen Peter up at Alert when he was on his way home from his second journey to the North Pole as a guide to a Japanese university expedition. I remember so clearly how he had begged me to teach him how to navigate, so that he could lead his own expedition of 'native people' to the point his American grandfather claimed to have reached on 6 April 1909. And now both of these companions of mine (whose lives I had saved on many occasions – and they mine on so many more) were buried in shallow graves at Qaanaaq, in Northwest Greenland, just a few feet from each other.

And so, ironically, with the pack ice from the Arctic Ocean blocking our exit from the fjord, I finally came to my senses and admitted a 'quixotic defeat'. Yes, we could come back next year and take up the lance and tilt at icebergs once again; but never with the same blinding passion, for that, alas, was spent.

Although I had not realized it at the time, that moment when we gave up was the end of my active polar career. Sure, I went back to the Arctic several times, but never on a 'mission' or chasing some impossible dream. I even went to the North Pole again with Allan to make a film, and made a crossing of the Arctic Ocean; but this time the easy way – as a lecturer on a Russian icebreaker with some one hundred paying passengers on board, as they would say: 'because they had always wanted to take part in a truly great adventure'. I also went back to the Antarctic for ten southern summers on various cruise

ships as a guest lecturer, and this was an absolute luxury compared with the life I had known. I got to see many places I had been unable to visit as an explorer, and to refresh my memory of those scenes and settings that had been an important part of my life. And then, of course, there was the discovery that I had a talent for painting – and this opened up a whole new world to me.

A Tribute to Allan Gill

Meanwhile, Allan continued on his own life path (very different from mine, and yet, at times inextricably linked). I was therefore deeply gratified to read that the Queen in January 2004 had approved the award to Allan of a second clasp to his Polar Medal for 'Antarctic and Arctic exploration up to 1989' – a period spanning 30 years during which time he spent a total of 17 winters and 20 summers in the Polar World.

This must surely be one of the most impressive career records of any Westerner in the entire history of polar exploration and research. In terms of time and isolation, no one has spent longer north of latitude 80 degrees on the Arctic Ocean than Allan Gill, and I am immensely proud that he has been with me on three of my expeditions. These three expeditions include the 1,500-mile journey we made with dogs retracing the route of Dr Frederick Cook from Greenland to Devon Island in 1966–67; the historic first surface crossing of the Arctic Ocean in 1968–69 (a journey of 3,800 route miles from Point Barrow, Alaska, to Spitsbergen via the Pole of Inaccessibility and the

North Pole – for which Allan received his first Polar Medal); and our attempts in l978–80 to make the first circumnavigation of Greenland. In the case of the last mentioned expedition (the most arduous and dangerous polar journey that either of us have ever made) I am the only witness to Allan's remarkable talent as a polar traveller.

His contribution to polar science, however, is much better known, for as a 'field man' he collected data from which several young and inexperienced polar scientists (over a period of some 30 years) wrote up their Ph.Ds. Looking back on their careers, all of these now-distinguished scientists know full well that without Allan's dedication and skill they would never have made it to the heady level of the International Conference Circuit. But of course none of them would now readily admit the debt they truly owe him.

On T-3 (a large piece of the Ellesmere ice shelf that for many years was floating around the Arctic Ocean) Allan was involved in the geophysical and oceanographic programme, seismic profiling, current measurements, water sampling, photographing the ocean bed, and dredging the floor of the ocean for mud samples. He also devised a method

Solitary Bear on Pack Ice (watercolour) [pages 123–24]

for taking core samples from the ocean bed sediments. On the pack ice camps his work was essentially the same, but added to that was the huge responsibility of being the only man with real life experience of living in that environment, and so he was constantly called upon to direct the scientists in hazardous and life-threatening situations. He was also responsible for selecting the ice floes on which these camps were established – again, calling on his experience of having been a member of the historic l968–69 British Trans-Arctic Expedition.

He was in the l970s a key man on the AIDJEX Project (the Arctic Ocean Ice Dynamics Joint Experiment), and later with shipboard oceanographic work in the Davis Strait and on the Arctic Ocean (where the ship was frozen in for the winter – as had been the *Fram* in Nansen's day). In all, a truly exceptional polar career, for which until recently he had received recognition for only one small part (a Polar Medal for his contribution as a member of the 1968–69 British Trans Arctic Expedition). It was therefore a delight for us both when he was honoured in May 2004 with the second clasp to his Polar Medal.

I shall never forget one particular moment Allan and I shared after a singularly difficult period in our last journey together; we had been hounded by fierce weather and were wretched with hunger and fatigue. As the storms tore at the tent and deafened us with unearthly howls, we had felt the ice beneath us move and break apart and saw the fear of imminent death mirrored in each other's eyes. It was a moment that profoundly scarred us both, and yet, a few days later, once the storms had ceased, we found ourselves in a wild paradise, never before seen by man. Allan turned to me and muttered: 'Don't for Chrissake ever tell anyone about this place.'

A pioneer has an unspoken responsibility to bring back something of value from one's travels – a map, a unique discovery, or specialist knowledge that contribute to mankind's understanding of our planet – but therein lies a dilemma: if one finds paradise, should one reveal its secrets to one's fellow man? It is not an easy choice. When one discovers a place of beauty one becomes responsible, in many ways, for its future, and mankind has a pretty poor record for treating our Earth with respect.

Now, as I look back, I feel it is timely to tell some of these stories in the hope that, through the reading or retelling of them, they instil some new appreciation and respect for this unique and fragile place – the Polar World.

Finally, with my leaning towards the mystical explanation for most of the mysteries we encounter in life, I leave you with the most enduring memory I have of the Polar World – which is of a recurring dream.

In this dream I was in a tiny hut – a 'padded tent' in the middle of the Arctic Ocean in the dead of winter. It was a familiar place, and with me were the same three companions with whom, in 1968, I had drifted through the long polar night, six black months of isolation, cold and constant danger. Suddenly in the dream there was a noise. It appeared to come from outside the hut and, strangely, the noise was made up of several sounds that produced the most terrifying scream I had ever heard. Whether it was the sound of ice breaking, or the wind, not one of us dared to guess, nor did it really matter, for what happened next almost stopped the heart beating. There was an 'explosion' – an almighty BLAST! But the door had not been blown in by the wind, nor even by the crescendo of sound. It had been blown in by LIGHT.

Wally Herbert   2001

Mother Bear and Two Cubs Sunbathing on Pack Ice
(oils)

'The mother bear and her two cubs off the north coast are sunbathing on the pack ice off the north coast of Svalbard. This is one of the main "denning" areas in Svalbard; but this particular painting has one other interesting feature — the island to the right is the one on which we landed at the end of our journey and its name was changed by the Norwegian Board of Geographic names in honour of myself.'

'The island to the right is the one on which we landed at the end of our journey and its name was changed by the Norwegian Board of Geographic names in honour of myself.'

Hunter & the Mirage (oils)

'This painting is of my old friend Avatak standing on a pressure ridge on Smith Sound. It is inspired by a scene I remember very well. In the distance, sea smoke is rising up off the water of a lead and breaking up a strange mirage.

'Avatak and I had been travelling with about five other hunters, when suddenly they went quite berserk as this mirage appeared – they could see it with their naked eye, but I had to use the binos. It was extraordinary – three bears were walking across the horizon, but as the horizon was blurred by the sea smoke it appeared as though the bears were walking across the sky, upside down.

'I remember very clearly the yellow colouring of the bears – distinctly different from the sky around them and the ice, and you couldn't mistake them for anything but bears. The hunters just threw everything off the sledges and shot off after them, and of course I followed. It was one of the most memorable moments I had with the Eskimo hunters.'

Shaman & His Dogs
(watercolour)

'Taitianguaraitsiak (right) was the old man who lived next to us on Herbert Island. He spoke only Eskimo and nothing else of course – and I had great difficulty understanding him much of the time, but some of his stories were told in such a way that I could understand. For example, he used to say that he didn't believe in Christianity, but he enjoyed the Christian imagery of angels, and this disturbed me, because I couldn't understand how he could believe in angels and yet at heart still be a shaman. Occasionally when we were out driving on his sledge he would point to an angel sitting on an iceberg, but he admitted later (when it flew away) that perhaps it was only a raven.

'The old man used to refer to himself as a little shaman because his father and his grandfather had both been powerful shamans. I asked him what spirit guides he had, and he answered that he had a black polar bear spirit, which in the winter would swoop down underneath the ice when he was going out across the sea-ice towards the open water to hunt walruses. It would swim underneath the ice, and would stop every time he stopped. Then, when he carried on, the bear spirit too would carry on. He knew it was there looking after him. Well of course it was very difficult to prove, but he was a charming old man, an absolutely lovely old fella.'

Solitary Bear on Pack Ice
(watercolour)

'This is a solitary bear – in fact, most polar bears are. But how can a painter show this? My answer is by giving the bear space to move – to avoid cluttering the scene with detail. So I have the bear walking into a clear ice field.'

Hunter & the Narwhal (oils)

'The Narwhal hunt is one of the most exciting in the repertoire of the Eskimo. The reason is that the hunter must, by order of the hunter's council, use the traditional method of the kayak and harpoon, which is extremely dangerous as the narwhal could easily capsize the flimsy craft. Here the hunter is waiting for the "Unicorn of the Sea" to pass him by – then he will paddle (as quietly as possible) up behind them, then alongside, from where he can throw his harpoon.'

'Sometimes when the sea is like glass and the hunter has been waiting for hours, motionless and mesmerized and soaking up the sun, he will have the strange sensation that he is floating not upon the sea but in the air between two worlds each of which is the undistorted image of the other.'

Wally Herbert, *Eskimos*, 1976

CHRONOLOGY

1934
- 24 October: Wally Herbert born in York. Childhood in Egypt and South Africa

1951
- Joins the army on a 22-year engagement with the Royal Engineers. Trains at School of Military Survey

1955
- Hitchhiked back to England from Egypt
- 27 December: sails from Southampton aboard the Royal Research Ship *Shackleton* for Hope Bay in the Antarctic ('Antarctica 1955–58')

1956
- Journey along the Graham Land Plateau with dogs
- 28 December: rescued from Cape Reclus
- Mapping on Livingston Island, South Shetlands, with dogs

1957
- Hitchhikes from Montevideo to London through South America, the United States and Canada

1960
- Arctic expedition in Spitsbergen with Hugh Simpson
- 18 June: meets the hunter of Moskushamn, who inspires him to cross the Arctic Ocean
- Summer 1960: journey up the west coast of Greenland to find dogs for the Antarctic

1961
- Transports dogs from Greenland to New Zealand, then down to the Antarctic for two years

1967
- 26 Feb–30 June: training in Greenland with Allan Gill and Roger Tufft. Sets out from Thule in extreme northwest Greenland to retrace Dr Frederick Cook's route with dogs across Ellesmere Island to Devon Island

1968
- 21 February: starts the British Trans-Arctic Expedition from Point Barrow, Alaska

1969
- 6 April: reaches the North Pole
- 29 May: completes first surface crossing of the Arctic Ocean
- 24 December: marries Marie
- Awarded Livingstone Medal by the Royal Scottish Geographical Society

1970
- 17 September: daughter Kari born
- Awarded Gold Founder's Medal by the Royal Geographical Society
- Awarded City of Paris Medal of French Geographical Society

1971–73
- Wally, Marie and Kari travel to northwest Greenland where they live with a small hunting community on Herbert Island for two years

1977
- Wins German State Literary Prize for his book *Eskimos*
- Winter: start of attempt at two years' circumnavigation of Greenland with Allan Gill

1978
- 30 March: second daughter, Pascale, born while on the circumnavigation expedition

1999
- Knighted for Services to Polar Exploration

Publications

1968 *A World of Men*
Eyre & Spottiswoode, London
1971 *Polar Deserts*
Collins, Glasgow
1971 *Across the Top of the World*
G.P. Putnam's Sons
1976 *Eskimos*
Collins, Glasgow
1978 *North Pole*
Sackett & Marshall, London
1981 *Hunters of the Polar North*
Time Life, Amsterdam

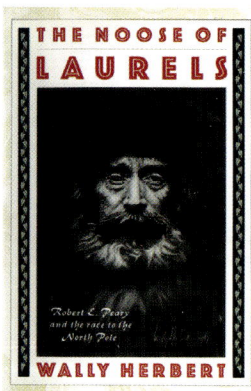

1989 *The Noose of Laurels*
Hodder & Stoughton, London, and Atheneum, NY
2007 *The Polar World*, London

Awards

Polar Medal and Bar
Gold Founder's Medal: the Royal Geographical Society
City of Paris Medal: French Geographical Society
Gold Livingstone Medal: the Royal Scottish Geographical Society
Explorer's Medal: Explorer's Club (New York)
Testimonial for a lifetime's contribution to Polar Exploration held at the Royal Geographical Society

INDEX

ACKNOWLEDGEMENTS

My deepest thanks to Kari, my daughter, without whose efforts and encouragement this book would never have happened. My profound gratitude also to Hal Robinson, who ran with the idea with unfailing optimism. Thanks are also due to Ali Moore and Peter Laws, who have helped bring this book to life. Finally I would like to thank my wife and greatest ally, Marie, who has been a constant source of strength, and who has held the vision for all my aspirations and endeavours.

Thanks to the following supporters of *The Polar World*:

John & Pauline Alderton	Simon Harris-Ward	Otto Norland
James Barclay	Ann Hawthorne	Mrs S.A. Peckham
Maggie & John Bilton	Doc Hermalyn	Patrick Pirie-Gordon
Ms Frances Bower	James Hewlett	Robert & Barbara Powell
Jason de Carteret	Miss Joyce Kemp	Guy Randle
Tarquin Cooper	Dr Margaret Leigh	Dave Reid
Dr Jonathan Craig	Raymond & Barbara Malony	Chris Rob
Mr & Mrs T. Crellin	Ray McGowan	Max Robinson
Sally Davidson	Martin McKay	Nick Russill
Carrod Dickenson	Mel McMahon	Frankie Ryan
Mandy Duncan-Smith	Lewis McNaught	Stephen Scott-Fawcett
Sir Ranulph Fiennes	Sidney & Joan Melman	Prof. Hugh & Myrtle Simpson
Peter Fuchs	Natalie Mills	Alan Tritton
Michael Gassaway	Nick Morgan	Nigel & Shane Winser
Pen & Mary Hadow	Simon Murray	Mrs V.H. Youell

Editor: Kari Herbert
Designer: Peter Laws
Proofreader: Ali Moore